THE
PREACHER'S PAPERBACK
LIBRARY

The Preacher's Paperback Library
Edmund A. Steimle, Consulting Editor

On
Prayer

Nine Sermons by GERHARD EBELING

Introduction by DAVID JAMES RANDOLPH

FORTRESS PRESS   •   PHILADELPHIA

Translated by James W. Leitch from the German
Vom Gebet by Gerhard Ebeling
J. C. B. Mohr (Paul Siebeck), Tübingen, 1963

© 1966 by FORTRESS PRESS

Library of Congress Catalog Card Number 66-17341

2718B66   Printed in U. S. A.   UB4005P

To Ernst Fuchs
June 11, 1963

ABOUT THE
PREACHER'S PAPERBACK LIBRARY

The renewal of the church in our time has touched many aspects of parish life: liturgy and sacraments, biblical and theological concern, the place of the laity, work with small groups. But little has been said or done with regard to the renewal of the church in the pulpit.

The Preacher's Paperback Library is offered in the hope that it will contribute to the renewal of the preaching ministry. It will not stoop to providing "sermon starters" or other homiletical gimmicks. It will, rather, attempt to hold in balance the emphasis which contemporary theologians and biblical scholars lay upon the centrality of proclamation and the very practical concerns of theological students and parish pastors who are engaged in the demanding task of preparing sermons of biblical and theological depth which also speak to the contemporary world.

To that end, the series will provide reprints of fundamental homiletical studies not presently available and contemporary studies in areas of immediate concern to the preacher. Moreover, because the study of sermons themselves can be of invaluable help in every aspect of the preparation of the sermon, volumes of sermons with introductory notes will appear from time to time. The sermons will include reprints of outstanding preachers in the past as well as sermons by contemporary preachers who have given evidence both of depth and of imaginative gifts in communication. It is our hope that each volume in The Preacher's Paperback Library, prepared with the specific task of sermon preparation in mind, will contribute to the renewal of the preaching ministry.

A host of volumes of sermons on the Lord's Prayer has appeared in print in the past. Is there any point in adding another? And especially as part of a series which addresses itself to the renewal of pulpit preaching?

There are two good reasons for adding this volume by Gerhard Ebeling to the list. First, it is written by a scholar who is deeply concerned for the primacy of proclamation in the light of the deep and perplexing hermeneutical problems of our day. David Randolph's scholarly introduction points to the problems and to the place of these sermons in the ongoing discussion.

Second, these sermons are pregnant with fresh provocative vistas into the meaning of prayer and into the implications of the specific petitions of the Lord's Prayer. But they are written in a style which precludes the lazy preacher from lifting them, warming them over with a few phrases and preaching them next Sunday. They provide the excitement of new and fresh insights along with the demand to bring these insights alive in terms of the daily experience of the preacher and his people. As such they may prompt the occasion for both preacher and people learning much that is new about the meaning of prayer.

EDMUND A. STEIMLE

Union Theological Seminary
New York, New York
Epiphany, 1966

AUTHOR'S PREFACE

In my occasional preaching in Zurich churches—at Witi-
kon, at the Fraumünster, and for the student services at
the Wasserkirche—I have for some time kept to the text of
the Lord's Prayer. The considerable lapses of time between
these sermons and the changing circle of hearers have not
permitted much continuity. Twice the date happened to
create a link with the Church Year—on both occasions in
the period before Christmas. Marks imposed by these external circumstances have not been subsequently retouched.
I have rather left it to the text itself to establish and preserve the inner connection.

I am aware of the problematical character of printed
sermons. Ernst Fuchs is right when he says: "God seeks
to speak with us not in writing but by word of mouth"
(*Gesammelte Aufsätze,* I, 106). Yet it seems to me appropriate to greet my older companion on the threshold
of his seventh decade with a gift which has grown out of
the preaching ministry. In our theological endeavors we
are both inspired by the conviction that the criterion of
theology is the sermon.

This fundamental principle is not meant to state a
party line; on the contrary, it is intended to declare war
on all theological party passions. We are, however, obli-
gated to allow the public to measure us by this criterion.
Thus not only is the printing of sermons justified, but even
the publishing of sermons which cannot by any means

claim to be homiletic models. It is my wish only that these printed sermons may serve to encourage the student of theology likewise to pursue his studies with an eye to the really burning question, so that on his own account he may then—*ubi et quando visum est Deo*—do justice to that question in a better fashion than is done here.

The non-theological reader, to whom this little volume is primarily addressed, should find in it a supplement to *The Nature of Faith* (Philadelphia: Muhlenberg Press, 1961), in which prayer, although not explicitly, was certainly implicitly discussed.

GERHARD EBELING

Pentecost
Zurich, 1963

CONTENTS

Introduction

IN NEW YORK'S METROPOLITAN MUSEUM OF ART one may find a fragile but luminous set of carved ivories which is all that remains of an ancient city. As a horde of attackers approached the venerable city, someone deposited these ivories in a well. Now that proud city and its conquerors lie unremembered in the dust while these discarded, rediscovered ivories continue to tell their story. The Lord's Prayer is not unlike these ivories. Uttered first with all the frailty of the human voice, attacked by enemies and discarded by doubters, this prayer still speaks when attackers and doubters are dumb.

In the sermons in this volume Gerhard Ebeling demonstrates the amazing delicacy and durability of the Lord's Prayer. The prayer is made up of "words"—mere, shimmering, shocking "words." Yet precisely here occurs the event in which God and man collide, and man's course can never again be the same. Professor Ebeling's study of this event and its consequences is so profound, provocative, and beautifully wrought that it seems destined to become a classic.

Few men of our age are as well prepared for the task of unfolding the meaning of this prayer as is Gerhard Ebeling, for whom this is the first volume of sermons to appear in English. Professor Ebeling, who at this writing teaches systematic theology at both Tübingen, Germany,

1

and Zurich, Switzerland, is regarded by many as our foremost contemporary theologian. "He will be to our future
what Barth and Bultmann have been to our past," proph-
esied Carl Michalson.[1] "Thank God, theological discussion
is alive again," Samuel Laeuchli exclaimed on reading that
work of Ebeling which is devoted specifically to theology
and proclamation.[2]

Words like these signal the emergence of an extraordinarily gifted man who has committed himself to the most
rigorous personal discipline for the sake of theology. Gerhard Ebeling was born in Berlin-Steglitz in 1912 and at-
tended the Gymnasium in Steglitz. In 1930-32 he studied
at Marburg with Rudolf Bultmann and others. He con-
tinued his studies in Berlin, then completed his doctorate in
Zurich under Fritz Blanke, his dissertation being on Luther's hermeneutics,[3] and significantly it is from *Luther*
that Ebeling gathered the connection between word and
faith which is so much at the center of his thought.

The young theologian served as a pastor in the years
1938-45, and his concern for the pastoral ministry was
not in the least abated when in 1946 he began to teach
church history in Tübingen. This continuing concern for
the church's ministry was made manifest in 1950 when
Ebeling took over the editorship of the important *Zeit-*

[1] Correspondence by Carl Michalson with the editors of Fortress
Press, Philadelphia.

[2] Samuel Laeuchli, Review of *Theologie und Verkündigung* by
Gerhard Ebeling, *Interpretation*, XVII (July, 1963), No. 3, 327.
This is a perceptive review, at once sympathetic and critical.

[3] Gerhard Ebeling, *Evangelische Evangelienauslegung: Eine Un-
tersuchung zu Luthers Hermeneutik* (2nd ed.; Darmstadt: Wissen-
schaftliche Buchgesellschaft, 1962).

Hereafter works cited in footnotes will be by Ebeling unless otherwise noted.

schrift für Theologie und Kirche, a "Journal for Theology and Church." In his first issue, the new editor wrote: "The situation that by and large critical historical research on the one hand and systematic theology and the preaching of the church on the other by-pass each other is the problem the Nineteenth Century left unsolved. It cannot be gotten rid of by dodging it or no longer seeing it. This danger is a present threat. It is to be opposed not only for the sake of the scholarly character of theology, but also—and this is not something different, but rather ultimately identical with the first—for the sake of the service, correctly understood, that theology is to perform for the church of the Reformation."[4] A theology which is critically constructive in regard to the church's task has consistently been the aim of Ebeling. This aim was further sharpened in the early Tübingen days by the personal friendship and scholarly dialogue between Ebeling and his New Testament colleague, Ernst Fuchs. In 1954 Ebeling became professor of Systematic Theology and Historical Theology at Zurich. In 1964-65 he was recalled to the theological faculty in Tübingen. He is presently on the faculties of both Zurich and Tübingen.

THEOLOGY AND PROCLAMATION

The devotion of this theological thinker to the profound simplicities of the Pater Noster reminds one of the statement that writing a good poem is like trying to carve the Lord's Prayer on a cherry stone. As in all sermons, theo-

[4] Translated for a brochure concerning "Journal for Theology and the Church: An Annual." This journal, on whose editorial board Ebeling sits, is published by Harper and Row as an English language counterpart and complement to the German publication.

logical immensities must be rendered in the simplest, most compact form. The simplicity and compactness of this work, however, must not tempt us to think that it is "minor," something the author "dashed off" in addition to his "serious labors." On the contrary, these sermons taken as a whole are not only the distillation of years of intellectual effort, but a positive advance in the author's total lifework. For "the vital factor" in the task to which Professor Ebeling is committed is precisely the tension between *theology* and *proclamation*.[5] The interdependence of theology and preaching[6] and the inability of one properly to function without the other make up the driving force in Ebeling's work.

Preaching has no greater contemporary theological champion than Ebeling. Nor has preaching a sharper theological critic than he. And it is important to understand both these points. Ebeling's writing is punctuated with lines in praise of preaching, such as these: ". . . Proclamation is the Alpha and Omega of ecclesiastical practice."[7] Proclamation is "the event theology exists to serve."[8] ". . . The criterion of theology is the sermon."[9]

There can be little doubt, however, when one frankly surveys the contemporary scene that God has gotten some

[5] *Word and Faith,* translated by James W. Leitch (Philadelphia: Fortress Press, 1963), p. 11.
[6] "Preaching" will be used in this introduction as a synonym for "proclamation" which is, for Ebeling, not only to be understood as the Sunday sermon but is not confined to it alone (see *Word and Faith,* p. 120, n. 3). What "true" proclamation and "true" preaching is largely makes up the subject of the present discussion.
[7] *Die Geschichtlichkeit der Kirche und ihrer Verkündigung als theologisches Problem* (Tübingen: J. C. B. Mohr [Paul Siebeck], 1954), p. 20.
[8] *Word and Faith,* p. 197.
[9] See above, p. ix.

low responses to his high calling. It is precisely Ebeling's lofty understanding of what preaching must be which causes him to be troubled about what passes for preaching in many pulpits. He writes: "Those who know what is really to be expected of preaching have surely of all people cause to be most deeply disturbed that so little happens, so little gets going, that so little is really understood here, that the sermon remains so remote, so unimportant, so non-committing. Despite all the theological arguments which lie to hand, the common complaint is simply true: it has so little to do with life, it remains an optional extra, *it does not get to the root of reality.*"[10] This comment is not uttered by a grandstand quarterback who merely observes from afar, but by one who preaches and confesses that his own preaching too often has fallen short. If we were fully honest, few of us would dissociate ourselves from Ebeling at this point.

Most of us who preach think that we would like to do so in a more authentic, responsible, and effective manner. The rub comes with the question whether we are serious about getting at the source of our trouble and setting it straight. Those willing to join this quest will want to familiarize themselves with the route traveled by Ebeling— a route which moves by way of the "new hermeneutic" through an understanding of reality and language, history, the question of the historical Jesus, and the word of God.

THE NEW HERMENEUTIC

The new hermeneutic is a movement rather than a school and hence is open to new configurations and differ-

[10] *Word and Faith*, p. 198, italics added.

ing interpretations.[11] Its presiding image is that of Hermes (Mercury), the messenger of the Gods. *Interpretation* is its principal function, and the conviction that the Bible can tell us what it means to be a man in the modern world suggests its major direction.

The "newness" of this hermeneutic arises from the dramatic turn in the understanding of interpretation which originates from such sources as Martin Heidegger. A further distinguishing factor is the specific question as to how preaching is to use the Bible as its text.[12]

Gerhard Ebeling and Ernst Fuchs of Marburg are preeminently associated with the movement on the continent. In this country a host of theologians have not only helped give Americans access to this development but have kept it moving and opened up new directions. In fact the "consultation on hermeneutics," presided over by Stanley Romaine Hopper, which draws together masters from different fields of specialization to discuss basic issues, is a way of doing theology which is no small part of the contribution made by the movement.[13]

In general, it may be said that the new hermeneutic has

[11] Among the basic books on the subject are Volumes I and II of "New Frontiers in Theology," eds. James M. Robinson and John B. Cobb, Jr. Volume I is entitled *The Later Heidegger and Theology* (New York: Harper and Row, 1963), while Volume II is entitled *The New Hermeneutic* (New York: Harper and Row, 1964). *The Drew Gateway* (Drew University; Madison, N. J.) devoted its Spring, 1963, issue to the subject in a valuable fashion. *Language, Hermeneutic and Word of God,* by Robert W. Funk, to be published soon by Harper and Row, will contain a number of illuminating essays on this subject.

[12] Ernst Fuchs in James M. Robinson and John B. Cobb, Jr. (eds.), *The New Hermeneutic,* p. 239.

[13] See John B. Cobb and Robert W. Funk, "Consultation on Hermeneutics," *Christian Century,* LXXIX (June 20, 1962), No. 25, 783-784; and Robert W. Funk, "Logic and the Logos," *Christian Century,* LXXXI (September 23, 1964), No. 39, 1175-1177.

opened up a corridor between Karl Barth's emphasis on "The Word of God" and Rudolf Bultmann's emphasis on the existential situation of man—a corridor which gains insight from them, yet moves on to new possibilities.[14]

Reality and Language

A definitive statement for the new hermeneutic is made by Ebeling: "The hermeneutic task consists for theology in nothing else but in understanding the *Gospel* as addressed to *contemporary man*. Whoever does not expose himself to the tension that entails, betrays both—the Gospel and contemporary man alike."[15] Here Ebeling draws together that which has often been separated—gospel and contemporary man—and declares that they are integrally related in the theological task. This declarative statement is important, but it is even more important to perceive the basis for it, namely, the understanding of reality. He writes: "It is not a case, rightly understood, of opposing tendencies that have to be brought to agreement in terms of compromise: concentration on the Word of God and consideration for the reality of the world. Rather, the Word of God embraces the reality of the world. The Christian is therefore not 'the man of eternal conflict.' 'His reality does not separate him from Christ; and his Christianity does not separate him from the world. Belonging wholly to Christ he stands at the same time wholly in the world.' "[16]

[14] *Word and Faith*, pp. 309-310. Cf. S. Paul Schilling, "Continental Theology Today," *Nexus* (Boston University School of Theology), IV (November, 1960), No. 1, 15-18, 35-40, 48 for a concise and incisive "placing" of Ebeling in relation to other continental theologians.

[15] *Word and Faith*, p. 11.

[16] *Ibid.*, p. 285. The quotations within the citation are from Dietrich Bonhoeffer.

Any attempt to drive a wedge between theology and persons betrays to Ebeling not merely a misreading of the current situation but a profound misunderstanding of reality. There cannot be one "reality" for the theologian and another "reality" for the man who must make decisions amidst concrete options which affect his future and that of others. Such a reality would be no reality at all. A better understanding has been expressed by a tailor who repairs his clients thoughts as well as their clothes: "Reality is what you have to face. You can't avoid it. You can't get around it. It's the way it is. It's the way it's going to be. You have to face it." This "layman's" view of reality is closer to that of Ebeling than idealisms which would project ultimacy beyond the range of the immediate encounters of everyday life. Ebeling puts it this way: "The German word for 'reality' (*Wirklichkeit*) brings out the fact that the real is one way or another something which is effective (*wirksam*), active, mighty, which has the capacity to impress as real, to assert itself and gain recognition as real, to concern man as real, and which, in that it contains possibilities and hence has capabilities, has a reference to the future."[17]

Theology does not speak only of God then as if he belonged to some exclusive realm of reality aloof from the conflicts and decisions of everyday life. Of course, theology does recognize God's transcendence over the processes of life, but this is not taken to presuppose a fragmented understanding of reality.[18] Theology, in fact, speaks of God and the world "not in unrelated juxtaposition, but in such a way that in speaking of God and of his revelation

[17] *Ibid.*, p. 379.   [18] *Ibid.*, pp. 403-404.

it has no other aim whatsoever than to speak correctly of the world, of history, of man, and thus of our reality—i.e., to speak of our reality in a way that is to the point. How to the point? Surely in such a way that this reality of ours is observed in the sense of being properly used and administered, and that this reality of ours is proved true in the sense that its appointed purpose is fulfilled."[19]

"The reality of God makes itself known only by revelation to faith"[20]—this Ebeling readily admits. He insists, however, that in the conflict about the nature of reality the church has a major point of contact with "non-believers," an insistence which Ebeling himself creatively manifests in his discussion with Martin Heidegger.

That the newness of the new hermeneutic is derived in part from Heidegger's insights is significant, for this philosopher has taken on no less a task than to complete metaphysics and thus put an end to metaphysics. The revolutionary character of Heidegger's enterprise is summed up by James Robinson: " 'Being' is not a fixed concept, but an occurrence that happens to us, something that dawns on us, and the various views about being that have been held over the centuries are the necessary result of the way in which being has on various occasions shown itself. This is a more primal grasp of the nature of thinking than is characteristic of the subject-object approach."[21] Heidegger has, furthermore, been a major tutor on the relationship of being and speech. As he puts it, "The being of man is founded in language."[22] He elaborates: "Language has the

[19] *Ibid.*, p. 197.   [20] *Ibid.*, p. 193.
[21] Robinson and Cobb, *The Later Heidegger and Theology*, p. 23.
[22] Martin Heidgger, "Hölderlin and the Essence of Poetry," *Existence and Being,* with an Introduction by Werner Brock (Chicago: Henry Regnery Company, 1949), p. 277.

task of making manifest in its work the existent, and preserving it as such. In it, what is purest and what is most concealed, and likewise what is complex and ordinary, can be expressed in words."[23]

Clearly, language is here regarded as something quite different from a series of signs and symbols by means of which persons deal with their environment. Heidegger admits that language of course does function to give information. But this ordinary sense does not exhaust the meaning of language nor even arise from its essence. "Language," he insists, "is not a mere tool, one of the many which man possesses; on the contrary, it is only language that affords the very possibility of standing in the openness of the existent."[24]

To those who have been living out their lives, earning their pay, and getting along with others by employing language in a certain way, Heidegger's claim comes as a shock. Nor would he wish it otherwise. He is convinced that a radical reinterpretation of language and being is absolutely necessary if we are to come to the truth. He has tugged at the slender roots of language, and the whole tree of theology shakes. The question may be put briefly. Does language "point" or does it "bring to expression"? Answer carefully, for an entire homiletical program is implied in the answer which is given, as we shall presently see.

Ebeling has no doubt been influenced by Heidegger's understanding both of being as *Dasein* and of the relationship between language and being. The decisive point of

[23] *Ibid.,* p. 275.
[24] *Ibid.,* p. 276.

difference between them is that when Ebeling hearkens to reality, he hears the word of God with all that this echoes of Jesus of Nazareth and the Christian church.[25]

History

There is a turn here toward understanding being in historical rather than non-historical modes which is crucial for Ebeling. He sees modern man as a Midas whose touch turns everything to history.[26] And, we might say, the man who touched Midas was Jesus of Nazareth. Christianity is the chief source of man's historical self-understanding. Ebeling is in basic agreement with Carl Michalson that "in Christ God has turned the world over to man,"[27] as he is with Friedrich Gogarten in holding that it is biblical faith which initiated the understanding of the primacy of history.[28]

Jesus Christ is the event which ends the domination of the past over man and sets him free to shape his future. Through Jesus Christ man knows that he is not at the mercy of supernatural forces and divine furies, but that he is responsible for the world. Freedom is the correlate of history, for to be a historical creature is to be free to choose one's past and to direct one's future. Recognized or not, Jesus Christ is the prism who suffuses modern man in the colors of history.

Yet Ebeling regards it as ominous that Christian faith

[25] *Word and Faith,* esp. pp. 324-332.
[26] *Ibid.,* p. 363.
[27] Carl Michalson, *The Rationality of Faith* (New York: Charles Scribner's Sons, 1963), p. 138.
[28] See Friedrich Gogarten, *Verhängnis und Hoffnung der Neuzeit —die Säkularisierung als theologisches Problem* (Stuttgart: F. Vorwerk, 1953); and *Demythologizing and History* (London: SCM Press, 1955).

has been captured by conceptions which actually prevent Christianity from seeing its own ground. He senses that Christian faith by and large has not been aware of its own unique character nor has it explicated its thought in these terms. His own work may be regarded as an attempt to reverse this trend.[29]

Nowhere is the spectrum of history more widely and vividly presented than in preaching. It is in his study of the historicity of the church and its proclamation that Ebeling deals in detail with "the major task of the pastor, proclamation, and indeed with proclamation in its concrete form as sermon in the Sunday service of worship."[30] "Historicity" never loses relationship to the event of Jesus Christ as Ebeling employs the word to become a multi-layered term operating on the following levels in regard to the sermon.

1. The priority of the biblical text. The text from Scripture is the fundament of the sermon; this is axiomatic. The preacher did not produce it; it is not the object of his wishes or desires. It comes to him from the past.

2. The text comes from a *particular* historical milieu. It was not dropped in a package from the sky, but arose amidst the struggles and hopes of a specific people at a certain time and place. Thus the text must be studied in

[29] See Carl Michalson, *The Hinge of History* (New York: Charles Scribner's Sons, 1959) for a pioneering work in "theology as history." Michalson's work is perhaps the most conspicuous and convincing attempt to swing theology into its native orbit of history and to chart the significance of this movement. See also Harvey Cox, *The Secular City* (New York: Macmillan, 1965) where "theology as politics" is suggested as a consequence of secularization. Cox refers to the work of Ebeling and Michalson on pp. 248-257.

[30] *Die Geschichtlichkeit der Kirche und ihrer Verkündigung als theologisches Problem*, p. 8. This discussion of the historicity of the sermon is drawn largely from Chapter I, pp. 5-30, of this work.

relation to these backgrounds, and this calls for the aid of biblical archeology and related studies.

3. The text comes from a linguistic tradition, and every language has its own "spirit." Therefore, understanding this text means coming to terms with the language of the original.

4. The text carries with it a tradition of interpretation. This is present in the "translation" from one language to another (i.e., from Aramaic to Greek to English for certain passages of the New Testament). Further, particular ecclesiastical traditions (i.e., Roman Catholic and Reformed) must also be taken into account since they affect not only the interpreter but his hearers.

5. The congregation to which the text is to speak is drenched in history. It cannot be wrung dry of its time consciousness to hear some abstract, "timeless" truth. Every sermon is a unique, one-time, unrepeatable event.

6. Yet, when all this study has taken place the sermon must not deal with the text as an archaic source but as a present word of God to the hearers. Indeed, critical historical research into the text is not to parade itself into the sermon, but to liberate the intention of the text to become contemporary address.

This contemporaneity in no way eliminates the historicity of the text but opens up new dimensions. Indeed, a sermon is not truly historical when it is merely a repetition of what has been said in the past. A sermon is not truly historical when it tells us only what the text *said*. The sermon must tell us what the text *says!* Lack of knowledge of the philosophical and poetic phenomena of the time and of the time's acute political or social problems are signs that the task of translation has not been placed in its full span. Historicity has not been taken seriously, and hence the exposition will fail.[31] The text is not understood in its full historicity until it speaks to contemporary man. Here the inner connection between history and hermeneutics is evident.[32] Furthermore, the text is not really *historical* until it is *interpreted.* Similarly, the relation between hermeneutics and preaching is clear, for the text is word of God, not as text, but as preached, interpreted text.[33]

The text is fully historical when through the sermon delivered in relation to it God speaks to contemporary men in their history and leads them into a new history.[34] The sermon thus is not the cataloging of the past but the creation of a future.

The priority of the text, its origin in a particular past, its language, its tradition of interpretation, the uniqueness of the historical moment, the present situation, and the future which is opened—these elements taken together express the historicity of the sermon. Preparation for preaching must take all these into account together with the event of Christ which animates them. And inasmuch as the text becomes word of God through the interpretation of the sermon to a particular congregation, we have here also the ground of the historicity of the church as such.[35]

Church history on this basis is to be seen as the history of the interpretation of Holy Scripture. Ebeling sums up

---

[31] *Ibid.,* pp. 24-25.   [32] *Ibid.,* p. 29.   [33] *Ibid.,* pp. 14-15.
[34] See *The Nature of Faith* (Philadelphia: Muhlenberg Press, 1961), p. 31; cf. pp. 21-30.
[35] *Kirchengeschichte als Geschichte der Auslegung der Heiligen Schrift* (Tübingen: J. C. B. Mohr [Paul Siebeck], 1947), see esp. p. 21.

the historicity of the sermon which also grounds the historicity of the church: "Because the word of Holy Scripture is a historical one, because the proclamation is a historical procedure, because the man toward whom the proclamation aims is with his world historical, for these reasons the sermon must be interpretation, and therefore interpretation must always be carried out and the sermon always be made new."[36] Where the text does not reach into the present, the sermon is crippled.[37]

The Question of the Historical Jesus

Gerhard Ebeling has inevitably been deeply involved in the discussion of the "new quest of the historical Jesus" with which the new hermeneutic has been associated.[38] "Christianity stands or falls with the tie that binds it to its unique historical origin,"[39] he states. Coming across this statement the casual reader might assume that Ebeling was simply repeating a cliché which is too often based upon a dichotomy between "history" and "faith." On the one hand there is the research on the "historical Jesus" which deals with his experiences up to the boundary of death. On the other hand, there are the confessions about the "Christ of faith" which refer to one who has crossed that boundary. Actually, Ebeling does agree that between these points of view there is a genuine tension which is

---

[36] *Die Geschichtlichkeit der Kirche und ihrer Verkündigung als theologisches Problem,* p. 24.

[37] *Luther: Einführung in sein Denken* (Tübingen: J. C. B. Mohr [Paul Siebeck], 1964), p. 102.

[38] See Ernst Fuchs, *Zur Frage nach dem historischen Jesus* (Tübingen: J. C. B. Mohr, 1960), which appears in English entitled *Studies of the Historical Jesus;* and James M. Robinson, *A New Quest of the Historical Jesus* (London: SCM Press, 1959).

[39] *Word and Faith,* p. 28.

not to be glossed over. The tension is already present in the name "Jesus Christ" which brings together views of an individual man and the work of God which was performed through him.

The more than casual reader will perceive, however, that this tension does not end the discussion by any means. As we have seen, the "historical" for Ebeling is not a simple, one dimensional category. The historical which gives rise to Christianity is not a "fact" or a set of facts back there somewhere which are to be collected and commented upon. Rather, it is an event which is to be shared and interpreted. This is said not as a concession to faith and dogmatics, but because of the character of the historical.

The properly historical question then is, "What came to expression in Jesus of Nazareth?"[40] And the answer is *faith*. "Faith," to be sure, is a word which misuse and overuse has worn thin, but we cannot for this reason deny its centrality in the biblical witness, its integral connection with Jesus, and its absolute necessity for life itself. In Ebeling's study of the phenomenon of faith,[41] he discerns the following structural aspects: (1) Faith is "existence in certainty"; (2) faith is "bringing about the future"; (3) "faith is power"; (4) "faith takes place in the encounter with other men"; (5) faith is "related to a concrete situation"; (6) faith is "always saving faith, indeed it is salvation itself."

To say that faith comes to expression in Jesus is to make no less a claim than that in Jesus, "God became Man in order that we through him may become real."[42] Ebeling's

[40] *Ibid.*, pp. 288-304, esp. 295-298.   [41] *Ibid.*, pp. 238-246.
[42] *Ibid.*, p. 200.

Christology is further explicated in his view that through his resurrection Jesus, who was the witness to faith, becomes the basis of faith.[43]

The Word of God

Theologically speaking, hermeneutics is the doctrine of the word of God.[44] It is at the point of Ebeling's understanding of the word of God that this whole discussion of reality and language, history and the question of the historical Jesus, converges on the preacher who confronts people—whether in or out of the pew.

Christian faith is faith in Jesus Christ. As such, "it is dependent on the tradition about Christ and hence upon the Bible."[45] ". . . the decisive thing in the Bible is the witness to Christ."[46] To say that the word became flesh (John 1:14) means that "here word became event in a sense so complete that being word and being man became one."[47] Interpretation of the Bible as the word of God is necessarily christological interpretation because Jesus Christ is the revelatory event, God's definitive word. Preaching is called for because it is here that Jesus of Nazareth is declared to be the present Lord, "according to the Scriptures."

The preacher's role is crucial, for "the biblical texts would not be rightly heard unless they were seen to present us with the task of proclamation."[48] Moreover, it is the word of God as proclaimed which provides the point of orientation for the church,[49] and along with the sacraments makes the church its true self.[50]

[43] *The Nature of Faith*, pp. 44-71.
[44] See *Word and Faith*, p. 332.
[45] *The Nature of Faith*, p. 32. [46] *Ibid.* [47] *Word and Faith*, p. 325.
[48] *Ibid.*, p. 329. [49] *Ibid.*, p. 121. [50] *Ibid.*, p. 185.

This sounds very traditional—and it is. But the new hermeneutical understanding quickens the material in a striking and fecund way which Ebeling is convinced is utterly in keeping with the Reformers' original intention. This becomes clear when Ebeling begins to define the term, "word of God": "Whatever precise theological definition may be given to the *concept of the Word of God,* at all events it points us to something that happens, viz., to the movement which leads from the text of holy scripture to the sermon ('sermon' of course taken in the pregnant sense of proclamation in general). As a first definition of the concept of the Word of God the reference to this movement from text to proclamation will suffice. For this is in fact according to Christian tradition the primary place of the concept of the Word of God."[51] The word of God is not a thing (an object, something "out there" to be caught and tightly held) but an event (a happening, an occurrence) in which men are addressed and put on the move.

The biblical text continues as the point of origin of the sermon. But in Ebeling's words: the sermon is not an *exposition* of the text but an *execution* of the text.[52] Now the cruciality of how we understand language becomes manifest. If language is merely a "tool" which "points" then the sermon must be understood as discourse about its object. But if language "brings to expression," then the word itself performs a hermeneutic function, and the sermon is the event in which man is brought to stand in the reality of God. In the latter case, the goal is not primarily

[51] *Ibid.*, p. 311.
[52] *Ibid.*, p. 331.

1. Ebeling's claim that "our place in the history of religion" is determined by atheism[65] is open to serious question. This is not to deny the message implicit in the "death of God" theme. However, it should always have been clear that once one says, "God is dead!" he should immediately add, "Long live the gods!" In our time the "death" of the one, true God has spawned a family of many false gods. Thus it may be claimed that polytheism is really the key factor in the consciousness of our time, and this has great significance for the strategy of preaching and the apologetic task.

2. With all the talk about "concreteness" a certain abstractness persists in much of the hermeneutical discussion. To be sure, this is largely due to the nature of the discussion which often seeks broad, underlying, general clues. Nevertheless, the relationship between hermeneutics, culture (in the sense of "popular culture," and in the sociological and anthropological senses), and politics needs exploration.

Also in regard to the sermons in this volume there is a serious question as to whether the preacher bears down sharply enough on the concrete meaning of the obedience called for by the text. This is not to suggest that the preacher is to become a political commentator nor a dispenser of prescriptions for behavior. But it is to suggest that preaching today requires more direct dealing with the implications of the text for social life.

3. The sermon in the context of formal worship needs

Heaven and Earth: Conversations with American Christians, trans. John W. Doberstein (New York: Harper and Row, 1965), pp. 39-58.

[65] *Word and Faith,* pp. 340-344.

further, positive treatment. To be sure, this is not the only place where preaching takes place. But as Ernst Fuchs puts it, "our ecclesiastical preaching" is deserving of much fuller discussion.[66] This discussion should consider the use of the Bible not only in preaching but in all aspects of worship, the general context of worship, and most especially the relationship of word and sacrament.

4. Other philosophical methods could be of more service to hermeneutics than is now apparent. Linguistic analysis, for example, can perform a useful ancillary service particularly in the observation of how words function in certain contexts. This is said with full awareness that there are deep and important differences between the "first principles" of linguistic analysis and hermeneutics. But if Ebeling's claim that hermeneutics has today become the meeting place for theology and philosophy is to take on full meaning,[67] encounter at this point is necessary.

5. The treatment, or lack of treatment, of the Old Testament in both the formal treatises and in these sermons leave important concerns uncovered. Ebeling's essay on "The Meaning of Biblical Theology"[68] is stimulating but brief, and his view of the Old Testament in general and *Heilsgeschichte* in particular is more implied than clearly stated. Ebeling no doubt has more to say in this area, and it will surely contribute to the discussion when he does so.

Allowing for unfinished business, the substance of Ebeling's views offers a full agenda for the renewal of preaching. The vitality with which Ebeling's total theological

---

[66] James M. Robinson and John B. Cobb, Jr. (eds.), *The New Hermeneutic*, pp. 237-238.

[67] *Word and Faith*, p. 317.

[68] *Ibid.*, pp. 79-97.

task expresses itself in his preaching is a further asset to which we now turn.

On Prayer

How does the understanding of preaching which we have just outlined come to expression in Ebeling's own sermons? Before we attempt to answer this question in terms of the sermons in this volume we must make it clear that these sermons are not intended to be "models" held up for imitation. They are *sermons*. As such they are to be listened to for the word of God which speaks through them, and our critical comments should be expressed in terms of this sound. Furthermore, comparisons made with Ebeling's other works are not to be used for a literalistic scorekeeping between what the author "says" and what he "does," between his "theology" and his "actual preaching." To raise the question of consistency is simply to underline the continuity between Ebeling's more formal treatises and his sermons as *one thoroughly theological enterprise:* to interpret the gospel as addressed to contemporary man. Finally, this sketch of some of the salient features of these sermons is not intended to cover the sermons with a blanket commentary but only to suggest some clues which hopefully will facilitate the reader's appreciation of them in relation to Ebeling's total contribution.

Aim

The aim of these sermons is suggested by the line: ". . . that what Jesus did then [in teaching the disciples to pray] ought also to happen now in this sermon in the working out of this text."[69] This means not that the

[69] See below, p. 44.

preacher is to assume the role of Jesus, but that through the sermon the text will help preacher and congregation to share in the event of being taught to pray by Jesus.

The aim of these sermons then is *event*. It is not the recitation of past data. It is not the distribution of information. It is not the shaping of an aesthetic entity. It is not the attempt to make us feel better. No, the aim of these sermons is *event,* which means that through the words of the preacher personally spoken to the congregation, the intention of the text awakens faith and gets the people moving in obedience to God's will. This corresponds to the aim of preaching set forth elsewhere, namely "to expound with the help of the text the reality which presently concerns us, i.e., to bring it to expression in truth and so bring the text to execution as a present word-event . . ."[70]

Text

"For a sermon text is a text from which help is to be expected."[71] The text is to help the preacher preach, and through the sermon to help the hearers to live.

This language is deceptively simple since a complex task of interpretation is involved if the help which is expected is actually to arrive. The preacher admits at the beginning of the series that frankly the text is an inconvenience to the preacher! This is because the text obliges us "to say not what we like but what is necessary . . ."[72] Furthermore, the text is inconvenient in that to understand it we must know its original background and its biblical context as well as its history of interpretation.

[70] *Word and Faith,* p. 431.
[71] See below, p. 39.   [27] *Ibid.,* p. 40.

One of the most striking features of Ebeling's deployment of scholarship is his modesty. Deftly he introduces just enough background information to be illuminating without drawing attention to itself. For example, Ebeling points out bluntly that we know "next to nothing" about the external circumstances in which Jesus' instruction in prayer took place. But he does discuss the difference between the accounts of Matthew and Luke.[73] Comments on the historical and philosophical backgrounds of the text are also brief and have the quality of a cameo, as does, for example, his discussion of Jewish and pagan presuppositions about God.[74] Similarly, most of the study of the original languages remains beneath the sermon except where it is crucial to understanding, as it is in the observation that the word Jesus used for "father" is "Abba," which is not a designation of a role but address to a person.[75] Likewise, study of the history of interpretation is mostly hinted at, although the references to Luther are telling.[76]

Each of these sermons is conscientiously bound to its text, but is not for that reason disconnected from the congregation.

Structure

Structure should be a function of the subject matter of the sermon rather than an abstract form into which material is poured. Ebeling's sermons demonstrate this premise, which is contrary to a good deal of homiletical theory.

Preachers are familiar with the convention which holds that every sermon should have an introduction, points (preferably three), application, and conclusion, the parts

[73] *Ibid.*, pp. 43-44. [74] *Ibid.*, pp. 48-49.
[75] *Ibid.* [76] *Ibid.*, p. 129.

of which are to be of equal length. No doubt this form is useful for developing many texts, and in fact this volume's sermon on "Give Us This Day Our Daily Bread" is of this order.

However, the subject matter does not always lead in this direction, and a variety of other structures are more typical of Ebeling's sermons. Among the constant factors there tends to be a longish introduction in which the preacher dwells on the text and probes it for understanding. Several possible approaches to the heart of the text may be essayed in the introduction. Further, the relevance of the text to daily life may be explored here since it is part of the understanding of the text itself, rather than a separate "application" of it. Once the intention of the text is clear, the preacher tends to strike off briskly and concisely the major points which emerge. The final point may itself be "summary" in character, or a very brief concluding statement may be made. One of the sermons concludes with a familiar hymn.

The structure thus consistently follows the function of the quest for understanding the text. They explore. They question. They express. Mostly asymmetrical in form, they are not formless, and Ebeling is not to be confused with those antisermonic preachers who merely share their feelings. Though unconventional, the structure is always there, serving the understanding of the text.

Point of Contact

The point of contact between these sermons and contemporary life lies in man's self-understanding. The "help" which comes from the sermon is ". . . that it causes man to come to himself by causing God to come to him."[77] For man to come to himself he must be concerned with that which is absolutely necessary for his life. Consequently "religious exercises" which are optional and superfluous are out. Rather, that which is absolutely necessary for life is—the word.

This will come as a shock to those who are used to speaking of "mere words" and regarding them as the very antithesis of something happening in their lives. But it is no surprise to one who has reflected upon the matter. Jean-Paul Sartre in his autobiographical work, *The Words,* describes how for him "finding himself" and learning to write came together. By writing he was existing.[78] Words were like commandments sewn into his skin. If he went a day without writing, or wrote too easily, the scar burned.[79] We are all galley slaves of language, Sartre concludes, ineradicably tatooed by words.[80] To say "mere words" is to say "mere life." Ebeling writes, "For a single word, when it takes place, can lay complete hold of us and carry us through everything—into the darkness, certainly, yet with the irrefutable expectation that darkness is not dark to thee."[81]

Self-understanding comes when word-event takes place in preaching. This event is marked by several characteristics. First, one learns the "right" word—the true, the authentic word. Sermons are the "language school" in which the Christian learns to name the experiences of life. Secondly, the word of preaching is heard as *my* word, one's

---

[77] *Ibid.,* p. 41.
[78] Jean-Paul Sartre, *The Words* (New York: George Braziller, 1964), p. 153.
[79] *Ibid.,* p. 164.   [80] *Ibid.*   [81] See below, pp. 57-58.

own personal expectation. For example, when "Father" is heard not as a title for God but as the address by which we pledge ourselves as his children, then the world turns a different face toward us. Thirdly, the hearer brings his life into agreement with the intention of the text: "Our human word is true word when it is response."[82] When our lives are lived out in line with God our Father, which is in love with our fellow man, word-event not only happens, it is also passed on to ever new life.

Self-understanding through word-event is thus the point of contact for the sermons, making for each text the distinctions necessary for us to understand our right relation to reality. A further reference to our understanding of the words, "Our Father," serves as a summary illustration. When we address God as "Father," then we know, "We are sons—not slaves, not prisoners, not condemned criminals in the death-cell of this world, but free men who are summoned to life, who have a future before them because they have God before them."[83]

Subject Matter

It would seem self-evident that the subject matter of these sermons is the Lord's Prayer. However, if what has been said about hermeneutics is in fact operative the prayer is not an "it," an object "out there" to be grasped and handed on to others. Rather, in the act of approaching the text as a source for self-understanding, a process of interaction between text and preacher takes place. Through what is known as "the hermeneutical circle,"[84] the text illumines one's self-understanding, and one's illumined self-

[82] *Ibid.*, p. 51. [83] *Ibid.*, pp. 51-52.
[84] See *Word and Faith*, pp. 321-322.

understanding enables one to perceive meaning in hitherto darkened corners of the text. The sermon becomes then like the musical composition of Abt Vogler in Browning's poem:

> That out of three sounds he frame, not a
> fourth sound, but a star.[85]

In reading these sermons one should be prepared for the "new" quality of the subject matter, which "newness" is not sheer innovation but the original intention of the text in our changed situation. For example, if the phrase, "Our Father, who art in heaven," is not demythologized but taken in a literalistic attempt to locate God in cosmic space, the result is the exact opposite of the text's intention which is to claim God's nearness to us in prayer. Furthermore, such mythologizing only perpetuates the notion that Christianity is tied up with outmoded and ridiculous world views. But if the intention of the text is appropriated in terms of our self-understanding we have a different story. Ebeling puts it this way: "To proclaim God as the God who is near, as Jesus did, is to put an end to the idea of heaven as God's distant dwelling place and to reverse the relation of God and heaven. It is not that where heaven is, there is God, but rather where God is, there is heaven."[86]

Throughout this volume new worlds open on the reader as he perceives that these sermons are not only about the prayer, but about himself, and about the reality which underlies both.

[85] Robert Browning, "Abt Vogler (After He Has Been Extemporizing Upon the Musical Instrument of His Invention)," *The Complete Poetic and Dramatic Works of Robert Browning,* Cambridge Edition (Boston and New York: Houghton Mifflin and Co., 1895), p. 383.
[86] See below, p. 50.

Concrete Situation

The distinctive thing about a sermon is that it is an address to people in a specific place at a specific time. Whereas systematic theology seeks to understand aspects of faith in relation to the whole of faith, the sermon attempts to articulate God's word for a concrete situation—one which is particular, unique, and inimitable.[87]

The emblem of environment is on these sermons. Their tightly reasoned dialectic, the range of vocabulary, the concern with the sceptic, all suggest their origin in a university community. In fact, one of the ironies of these sermons to American readers who may be familiar with more "homey" sermons is that in preaching to an academic community one may have to abstract in order to be concrete. That is, speech at high levels of abstraction is typical in such cultures, and while this does not mark the scholar as a separate species of man it is a factor which must be taken into account in addressing him. A further sign of the environmental sensitivity of these sermons is their allusions to the *time* of the year, for example, Advent in the church year and the coming of the Christmas feasts in the "secular" calendar.

That sermons bear the mark of their place of origin by no means makes them totally alien to other situations, and this is certainly true of these sermons. To be sure, a pastor addressing his own congregation will develop a certain ambience, the shadings of which may be lost on those who cannot read between the lines—and this is not undesirable. But it is true that great preaching descends through the personal and strikes a universe. Thus we see

[87] *Word and Faith,* p. 431.

ourselves in these sermons and know ourselves judged and redeemed by their message.

Faith is not really faith unless it takes place in a concrete situation.[88] And faith means to perceive that concrete situation as one for which one is responsible and to act upon this insight. This is easily enough said. Yet there is probably no more vexing question today than how preaching is to speak redemptively to society. Nevertheless it is clear that we must make the attempt at such redemptive speaking or forfeit our right to speak at all.

Ebeling is one of those "postwar" continental theologians who has evidenced a genuine and pervasive concern about the relevance of theology to social issues. These sermons show evidence of this concern, although the references to social action are largely indirect. Among examples are these: (1) an extensive discussion of the fundamental relation of God's will to world events on pages 72-78; (2) a statement on poverty on pages 90-91; (3) reference to the problem of hunger and the "Bread for the World" program on page ??. However, it is not so much in these specific references as in Ebeling's underlying grasp of the reality which speaks to man's conscience and sets him free for responsible action that we see his major contribution in this area.[89]

Style

Every serious preacher has a style, a virtually indefinable "touch" which marks a sermon as his own. Ebeling's sermons are marked by the quality of control; he is a "cool"

[88] *The Nature of Faith,* p. 159.
[89] *Word and Faith,* pp. 413-423.

preacher even though the sermons are full of the stuff of everyday life. But perhaps Ebeling's style is most vividly captured in a phenomenon which recurs in the sermons which may be described in Henry James's phrase, "the turn of the screw." For James, a really good story had a *twist* to it which distinguished it and gave it vitality. In James's famous novel which bore the title, *The Turn of the Screw,* the governess speaks of the "shock of a certitude" which came over her. A "flash of this knowledge . . . for it was knowledge in the midst of dread" produced in her "the most extraordinary effect, starting . . . a sudden vibration of duty and courage."[90]

Reading these sermons one senses what James described, although independent of the supernaturalism found in the novel. We are reading along, covering language which is biblical, traditional, familiar. Then, suddenly, there comes the turn of the screw. The preacher has given a spin to the words which brings a flash of insight and sets us vibrating.

Where this happens will no doubt vary with the sensibilities of the reader. But the phenomenon is associated with that point where Ebeling restates a familiar conception in unfamiliar language. Of the new statement, he will say, "That sounds strange . . . ," or "It sounds ironical. . . ." But, Ebeling will continue, it leads us to the truth. Here are some examples of this phenomenon: "Strange as it may sound, it is a fact that we cannot simply ask God for this or that. We must first of all ask him for *himself.*" [91] "That sounds strange to our ears, because we

[90] Henry James, *The Turn of the Screw,* in *The Great Short Novels of Henry James,* ed. Philip Rahv (New York: Dial Press, 1944), p. 654.

[91] See below, p. 55.

associate *the conception of certain sacred letters* with the name of God, but not the *expectation of the Holy Spirit.*"[92] "It may sound ironical when I seek to justify the demand for this linguistic exercise by emphasizing that the helpful thing about the phrase 'time of God' is that it is difficult to form any conception of it."[93] "That sounds strange, and yet it is only compressing the sentence, 'Thy will be done, on earth as it is in heaven,' into a single expression: God-world-event."[94]

Ebeling observes: "Jesus had the audacity to speak of God and to God in such a way that to pious ears it sounded offensive, disrespectful, worldly."[95] Lines like those just noted display a daring like Jesus' own. This "turn of the screw" which releases new meaning operates in Ebeling's sermons like a signature, setting their style and identifying them as his own. In these moments, insight dawns. Understanding arrives. Word becomes event!

Hopefully this volume will help us not only to learn to pray but to learn to preach. If we turn to Gerhard Ebeling for help, however, we must be prepared for a shock since his scholarly manner is deceiving. He is rather like a supplicant who moves quietly through the cathedral gently placing dynamite at all the crucial spots. Then, with a courteous bow, he pushes the plunger. Yet it is undeniable that if our preaching is truly to become preaching of the word of God we must explode the fictions which surround it and start from the ground up. We must set out on a radical reinterpretation not only of preaching

[92] *Ibid.,* p. 57.
[93] *Ibid.,* p. 66.
[94] *Ibid.,* p. 73.
[95] *Ibid.,* p. 49.

but of the whole historical and conceptual framework in which preaching takes place. Gerhard Ebeling is superbly qualified both as demolition man and architect to aid us in this crucial task of understanding.

DAVID JAMES RANDOLPH

Drew University
School of Theology
Epiphany, 1966

On Prayer

Pray then like this:

OUR FATHER,
WHO ART IN HEAVEN

This text is intended to help us. Help us to what? The answer seems so obvious: it is intended to help us to pray. But is this answer, so obvious in itself, the whole answer? Our piety must not prevent us from being thorough! Ought we really to be content with the answer that the text is intended to help us to pray? Are we not compelled to press further and ask what help prayer is supposed to be to us? It sounds impious to ask that. But there is impiety here only when the question is not a genuine question which looks for an answer, but is already an answer which merely takes the form of a question. If we sincerely ask what help prayer is supposed to be because we do not know but long for an answer, then it is as if we were reaching out to this text not just with one hand but with wide open arms. And to stifle that movement would be impious.

But is it really the intention of the text to offer such far-reaching help? Although I began so matter-of-factly by saying that this text is intended to help us, that is certainly not a truth unique to this text. It is fundamentally true of every sermon text. For a sermon text is a text from which help is to be expected. We ask once again: help for what? It may sound somewhat pedantic, but although there is only one answer here it must be divided into two parts: the text is intended to help us to preach, and it is intended through the preaching to help us to live. We ought therefore to expect a very great deal from the text, and through the text from the sermon. Actually we most often expect precious little of either. And our experience of preaching and listening to sermons unfortunately seems to show we are right in expecting so little. What does happen here anyway? But perhaps the reason so little happens is that we expect so little—as listeners from the sermon, as preachers from the text.

There are kinds of help which suit our convenience. We are glad to welcome them. But there is also a kind of help which can be very inconvenient—the help which is designed to rouse us and to set us in motion. The event of preaching is of this kind. It is an inconvenience for the man who is to preach to have the text to assist him. Superficially, of course, it appears otherwise, for the text seems to provide the material without which we should have nothing to say at all. But on closer examination and rightly understood, the text actually makes preaching difficult for us by obliging us to say not what we like but what is necessary, and to do this not simply by repetition and mere illumination of the text but—appealing of course to the text—on our own account. That the text in this very way is actually a wonderful help is a thing which probably dawns on us in the preaching ministry only after many trials and tribulations; and it must be learned anew every time we preach.

This is also true in much the same way for the listener.

The divine service on Sunday morning is sometimes considered, even on merely external grounds, to be inconvenient. On such grounds one could of course also maintain the very opposite: that that is surely a very easy way to serve God! But such reflections remain superficial. The fact is that at the divine service help is to come—and precisely through the sermon. And I have said already that the text is intended through the preaching to help us to live. That is, it is not merely to contribute in one way or another to our instruction or our entertainment, to our spiritual edification or our moral rearmament. All these things may surely happen through the sermon. But in a much more radical sense the purpose for which the sermon takes place, the help which is to be expected precisely from the sermon, is that it causes man to come to himself by causing God to come to him. For of course the sermon is supposed to be God's word. But what else is God's word save God's coming? What we should expect from the sermon is that through it God approaches us and comes to us and that precisely thereby do we come to ourselves. This is vitally necessary. This is why the sermon is, in a very radical sense, help, but therefore also a most inconvenient help.

Today's text urges us to pray. That is help in the radical sense only when it does not urge us to a particular religious exercise but aids in bringing about what is absolutely necessary for life. The question which thrust itself upon us was therefore quite in order: what help is prayer meant to be to us? For the point at issue is: what does prayer have to do with the one absolute necessity of life? And the critical question regarding our preaching was also entirely justified: what does happen here anyway? And now in regard to this text we may ask: what really happens when we are urged to pray? If it is really a case of that which is necessary, then we must relentlessly ask what *happens*. For where nothing happens, we are obviously a long way from that which is vitally necessary.

The question, "What happens here anyway?" can in the present case be doubly embarrassing to us. For it applies not only to the sermon, but also to that which according to our text is the aim of this sermon, prayer. Wherever we turn, we have to do with words. The sermon—obviously, words. And prayer—also words. Mere words, one might say, and not happenings. To be sure, preaching and prayer are definite processes. We have to devote a certain amount of time to them, however modest that amount. So to that extent they are events. But once more: what *happens* where someone merely speaks? Our very bearing expresses the fact that now we cease working in order only to listen, that now we fold our hands—put them in fetters as it were—in order only to pray. It could of course be said that concentration of this kind is also intensive work, and furthermore a gateway to new activity. If anyone regards sermons and prayers merely as a chance to relax, and does not see them in themselves as activity related to all his other activity, then he has not the slightest idea of what is going on here. But even when we have pointed out all these things, we have not yet said enough. For the reason why preaching and prayer have to do with the one necessity of life, and therefore in the very highest degree with something that happens, is *precisely that* they have to do with words. Yet how are we to understand that it is precisely in words that such a decisive event takes place? The answer is, that this is true only when God and man encounter each other in the word. Where that happens, the absolute necessity of life happens.

Our text should now help to clarify matters. Short as it is, it has two parts. First: "Pray then like this." Formally, this is merely introduction, yet surely not for that reason unimportant. For it reminds us that Jesus taught men to pray. Of the external circumstances in which this happened, we know next to nothing. Matthew has taken this directive of Jesus concerning prayer and made it part of the great complex of teaching which we call the Sermon on the Mount. Luke has set it in the framework of a separate scene in which one of the circle of disciples makes the request: "Lord teach us to pray, as John also taught his disciples." The biographical detail is of no consequence. What is certain, however, is that Jesus did teach them to pray. That is striking, for his disciples were Jews, and a Jew knows how to pray. Why did Jesus have to teach them to pray? The fact that, as we are told, John the Baptist also taught his disciples to pray, shows that this was not altogether unusual. Those who know how to pray ought also to know that at best they are in the process of learning how to pray. This presupposes that God is taken seriously. But all praying takes God seriously. In the Sermon on the Mount the heathen are pointed to as a horrible example, not because they do not pray, but rather because they think they will be heard when they use a lot of words, and precisely this makes it clear that they do not take God seriously. Among the Jews too there was this kind of heathen prayer. It exists among us

43

Christians also. That is why there is always a place for instruction in prayer.

Whenever God is spoken of in such a way that God approaches us, the question of prayer acquires a new acuteness. All right proclamation is at bottom instruction in praying. Thus part of the peculiarity of Jesus and his proclamation is the special manner in which instruction in prayer took place. Our text is the result of that. For the fact that Jesus taught how to pray has become the source of all further instruction in prayer. And the fact that Jesus' injunction, "Pray then like this," is a part of the text of this sermon means that what Jesus did then ought also to happen now in this sermon, in the working out of this text. However, it is not now enough for me simply to repeat: "Pray then like this." For who am I, that I should have any private means of teaching others to pray? No, if I do in fact venture, not in competition with Jesus but in the execution of his will, to teach others to pray, then I can do so only in his name. But that means that I point not merely to the words which he has taught us to pray, but that I point to him as well, to the one who had the authority to give instruction in prayer.

And if I am now asked: "What really happens, then, when you preach about praying?" then I answer: What happens is, that Jesus himself approaches—not merely a single saying of his, a single piece of his instruction, but he himself in the unity and entirety of all that happened in his life and death. And what happened there? According to the Christian confession the decisive thing for all men of all ages happened in the life and death of Jesus. Our very method of dating expresses the fact that in Jesus

44

the decisive turning point took place. How so? The language of Christian proclamation has expressed the fact in
very different ways. Paul says: "When the time had fully
come, God sent forth his Son" (Gal. 4:4). In John's
Gospel it is put thus: "The word became flesh and dwelt
among us" (John 1:14). Elsewhere it is said in other
ways. But the point is always one and the same: in Jesus
God is come near. His own proclamation lays a finger on
this: "The sovereignty of God is come near." The path
he trod points the same way. That is why his whole being
was concentrated on one end: to awaken faith. And that
he taught to pray means the same thing. The purpose of
our text is to help us, by means of this sermon, to share in
that event.

That, however, is surely only to raise the fabulously
exalted claim that what is happening here and now is the
one absolute necessity of life. But whether and to what
extent this is really so is a question we must still ponder
with each other. For there is a common contempt for
words which is right in claiming that fine words achieve
nothing here. It remains completely true that the kingdom of God rests not on words but on power. Words,
however, remain fine, high-flown words so long as we are
not in agreement with them. So the vital thing is now that
here, since of course it is a question of Jesus, we should
learn to agree with Jesus.

Now it is to this end that the second part of our text
would help us. For in it Jesus says how we are to pray,
"Our Father, who art in heaven." We can agree wholeheartedly with these words, however, and through these
words with Jesus, only when we agree with what happens

in these words. For that reason we must turn our attention to what happens in prayer, and specifically to what happens when we pray as Jesus taught us. What happens when we call upon God as Father? We must be clear on two points here.

First, we are put in a position to speak a true, valid word at any time. Why that should be something good, helpful, and vitally necessary to life is, to be sure, something we understand only against the background of Jesus' warning against much speaking. That is, incidentally, equally true for the sermon. For in preaching and prayer it is a question of the right use of words. It could even be said that preaching takes place so that, ultimately and deeply, we may learn to speak rightly. And in prayer —to be sure, not only here, but here in the ultimate and deepest sense—it comes to light whether we have learned how to use words rightly, and indeed whether, when we are challenged to the utmost, we have anything at all to say or must remain dumb. If God's word takes place in the sermon and if the response to it takes place in prayer, then here man is indeed challenged to the utmost, because he is involved in his inmost being—in his conscience, in his heart—where the decision on man's nature is made. And so it could be said that the sermon and prayer constitute the real language school of man. It is all the more dreadful if room is given here of all places to a corruption of speech and the misuse of words, a symptom of which is a multiplying of words because of their devaluation. Nowhere is there so much sinning with and against words, as where empty, cheap, worthless words are used to speak of God and to God. Luther, who knew a thing or two about it, has said: "The right method is to use few words, but in many and profound meanings and senses. The fewer the words, the better the prayer. The more words, the worse the prayer. Few words and much meaning is Christian. Many words and little meaning is pagan." With that he hit exactly on what Jesus was after when he taught us to pray.

Jesus did not teach many words, but few, and these were full of weight. Indeed, to be precise, even these few words are at bottom only one. We call the prayer we have received from him the Pater Noster, the Our Father. It is also customary in other cases to cite texts and formulas by their opening words. Here, however, the opening already contains the whole thing. The seven petitions of the Lord's Prayer contain only what is expressed and takes place in this invocation. It is therefore well worth while clearly to realize that we can no longer reconstruct with certainty the exact wording in which Jesus formulated the Our Father. Luke has transmitted it in a somewhat different form than we are accustomed to in Matthew. But that is of no consequence, and does not in the least diminish our thankful wonder at the Lord's Prayer as it is now generally used: that such inexhaustible profundity is so briefly and simply brought to expression and made available for everyman. The important thing, as we have said, is not the individual words. Jesus did not seek to teach us a prayer, but to teach us to pray—and that of course means at the same time to liberate us from anxious and superstitious use of formulas.

The instruction in prayer is therefore already given in its entirety in the text to which we have restricted ourselves today: the invocation which is at the same time the sum of the whole. And even this is to be summed up in the one word, "Father." Whether the addition "in heaven" derives from Jesus is questionable and again a matter of indifference. Luke, at any rate, according to the better textual witnesses, has only "Father." And we know from Paul that the primitive Christians even in the Greek-speaking congregations used and handed on the Aramaic prayer, "Abba, Father." Meant as an invocation, this also signifies, "My Father, our Father." This is the point at which Jesus' instruction in prayer is concentrated: to give us the freedom in which at all times—even and precisely at a time when all words fail, when perforce they die on our lips and we become speechless—we can still say the one thing, the decisive, helpful, vitally necessary thing: "Father."

That brings us to our second point, and the whole thing seems to be upset again by an observation which must certainly not be quietly ignored. It is not by any means the case that Jesus was the first to designate God as Father nor the first to teach men to address him as Father. On the contrary, we find the name Father given to God already in Judaism, and indeed it is also so widespread in the realm of pagan religions that we seem to be dealing here with a kind of religious root word. Moreover, it can also be shown that every single line of the Lord's Prayer is already found in Jewish prayers. Nevertheless the whole breathes a new spirit. And that is true also of the invocation of God as Father. It goes without saying that the view of Jesus, along with that of Judaism, is to be sharply distinguished from the pagan view which sees the fatherhood

48

of God in terms of physical generation—that is, the idea which means by God the Father that he is the world's progenitor (for which reason the Stoics regarded theology as the crown and conclusion of physics). But even in comparison with Judaism a difference can be recognized—perhaps, indeed, even in the word "Abba." For "Abba" is not the most precise form of the word for "Father," but is presumably the baby talk of a child, containing all the nearness, affection, and love in which we do not *designate* a person as father but in which the child addresses its father. "Abba"—that was the expression heard from the lips of children in the secular language of every day. Jesus had the audacity to speak of God and to God in such a way that to pious ears it sounded offensive, disrespectful, worldly.

But now this "Abba, Father" is not an isolated term; it is rather a whole sentence. It is not merely a kind of colon so that the really important thing only comes after it; it is rather the heading which already contains the whole. The man who can wholeheartedly use the invocation "Father," has said all that is to be said. Hence the fact that the title Father is used for God in paganism and Judaism does not contradict the fact that something decisively new has taken place in the way in which Jesus taught men to say "Father." Paul, in whose heavygoing theology one does not really expect such a thing, confirms that this is in actual fact the sum total of the Christian faith. For the Holy Spirit, who is the Spirit of Jesus and therefore the Spirit of sonship, expresses himself in the one utterance: "Abba, Father" (Rom. 8:15-16; Gal. 4:6). That is the voice of the Holy Spirit. That is *the* word of faith.

We can speak thoughtlessly and in unbelief about God and to God as Father. The important thing is that we speak in faith, that is, that we allow these words really to be true, that we observe and embrace the truth that God is our Father.

This means to acknowledge the truth of God's nearness and to lay claim to it. If the phrase "who art in heaven" were meant to be understood as an expression of the remoteness of God, then we should actually have to worship in opposition to this addition. For the kingdom of heaven is come near. To proclaim God as the God who is near, as Jesus did, is to put an end to the idea of heaven as God's distant dwelling place and to reverse the relation of God and heaven. It is not that where heaven is, there is God, but rather where God is, there is heaven. Make what you can of that! And let us stop speaking of heaven altogether, if we cannot execute this change in thinking. To put it rather foolishly for once: it is better to lose heaven than to lose the nearness of God! For "Our Father, who art in heaven" means precisely, "Our Father, who art present here on earth." For the fact that God is near is not to be measured in terms of space. God is so near that he is nearer to us than we are to ourselves. Nor is the fact that God is near to be measured in terms of time. God is so near to us that he is constantly ahead of us, awaiting us and engaging us as our future.

With the one word "Father" we are allowed not merely to say this, but also to let it happen as we say it. It is a tremendous event when we take seriously the invocation: "Our Father." Who is it we are addressing here? No man, although in doing so we have all men in view. No earthly thing, although in doing so we also have in view everything in the world that concerns us and troubles us. "Our Father," we say in the midst of the world, under the buffetings of the whole world, and to that extent in the teeth of all the world. To whom? To a nonentity? In actual fact it *is* to that which bursts upon unbelief as the mystery of nothingness, striking it dumb in speechless horror. *That* is what we are permitted to address as Father, because what comes to us from that quarter is not nothingness, but is through Jesus the voice of the Father, and in that voice the Father himself with outstretched arms.

When we say, "Our Father," what happens is no less than that the world receives a different face as we hold fast to the fact that in Jesus the face of the Father looks upon us. We naturally think that words are meaningful only as a means of communication between men, and that it is therefore really foolish and meaningless to speak to God in human words. But to think that way is completely to fail to realize what is actually at stake in our words: no less than our true being. Where no word can be spoken, there everything is dark and meaningless, there death reigns. Praying is therefore a participation in the work of God, in the redemption of the world, in the process in which God's creation becomes true creation and we men become true men. Praying is a sign of the fact that where words are concerned God takes precedence. Our human word is true word when it is response. That this is how we come to be true men is brought out in the fact that as those who say, "Father," we are sons—not slaves, not prisoners, not condemned criminals in the death-cell of this world, but free men who are summoned to life, who have a future before them because they have God before them.

When we understand prayer in this way and learn to pray in this way, then the problem as to whether or not prayer is heard no longer exists at all. For what does it mean that the invocation "Our Father" is heard? Would that be a second thing supplementary to what happens when in faith we say, "Abba, Father"? Is not the very thing which happens when we say this the fulfillment and answer of all prayer: even the presence of the Holy Spirit, the nearness of God?

Yet all this is so easily said. Till our deathbed we have to work unceasingly at the one lesson: to learn to say with all our heart, "Abba, Father."

TWO

HALLOWED BE THY NAME

We are on the way towards Christmas, each in his own manner or his own way—or, more accurately, we are rushing madly towards Christmas, or perhaps even drifting towards Christmas while preoccupied with other things. It would be more fitting—we know this, and that is why we are here—to *look expectantly* towards it. Not, of course, in expectation merely of the feast which, to be sure, with all its familiar trimmings has its right and proper place. We would not here cast any puritanical doubts upon it. Once we are clear about the decisive thing, however, the rest can find its place in uninhibited freedom.

The decisive thing is *waiting on God*. That is what Advent means. And indeed that is still its meaning, even though we say at Christmas, "He *has* come!" Yet we certainly do not wait over and over again in artificially changing spirits, as if a mystery play were here to be annually repeated. On the contrary, since the birth of Christ it is always, and now more than ever, true that the decisive thing is waiting on God. Now, however, we wait with understanding. For Jesus brings us to understand what is to be expected from waiting on God. We can simply say he brings us to understand God and encourages us to wait on God, thus allowing that really to be the decisive thing.

It may be that we lack this ability to wait on God with understanding, courage, and decisiveness—lack it so completely that we cannot form any clear picture at all of what it means. We know of course that looking expectantly to God includes *praying*. And the man who waits on God will make that the chief petition of his prayer. The first petition of the Lord's Prayer is therefore an appropriate text for the days before Christmas: "Hallowed be thy name." It expresses pure waiting on God. It is, furthermore, in the historical sense a pre-Christmas, pre-Christian text. Jesus has here taken up something which every Jew prays.

But now, how is this particular phrase to bring us to understand the meaning of waiting on God? Perhaps it will do so if at the same time we have the Christmas message ringing in our ears. Christmas should enable us to understand this first petition better in the light of its *fulfillment*. And, conversely, this petition should perhaps give us a better understanding of Christmas. But does that not mean that one x is to explain the other x? For indeed both are at bottom very strange and very obscure— the first petition of the Our Father, although we all know this prayer by heart and have spoken it who knows how many times; and the Christmas message, although we have celebrated Christmas since our earliest childhood and are still bound to it by some mysterious tie. Yet both will perhaps begin to speak to us in a new way when we put them together.

Even though we do in fact feel that each of these two things is by itself hardly intelligible any more, it might help us if we notice how they are linked to each other

54

through *Jesus*. In him—so the Christmas message says—our waiting on God is *fulfilled*. By him—so the first petition of the Lord's Prayer reminds us—we are also *summoned* to wait on God. The two even become one. The fulfillment is here not the end of the waiting, as it normally is, but rather the start of true waiting on God. When God has come, when he has really dawned upon us, then and only then can we also arise to wait on him.

For where it is a question of God, no one is a possessor, but everyone is a *beggar*. That sounds like an exaggeration but is actually an understatement of the real truth. The man who begs has a partner to beg from, and needs only to beg for this or that from him. The man who *prays,* however, has actually to pray for the partner to pray to, and all other petitions take second place to that. Strange as it may sound, it is a fact that we cannot simply ask God for this or that. We must first of all ask him for *himself.* And what is even stranger: if we pray *to* God and therefore *for* God, then we must actually even pray *on God's behalf!*

We know that Jesus taught this as the right order in prayer: to think first exclusively of God's side—his name, his kingdom, his will, and only then of our side—our daily needs, our guilt, our perils, and our lostness. One can explain this by saying that God's affairs are infinitely more important than ours, even as his glory stands in infinite contrast to our afflictions. But that is only a half-truth and an inadequate explanation. The purpose of prayer is surely not to separate but to unite: to make God's cause ours and our cause God's.

Hence when our prayer begins, "Hallowed be thy

name," we ought not to tone down its amazing, and indeed offensive, aspect or reduce it to a mere act of reverent adoration before the glory of God. For this is *the most necessary petition.* In other words, it is concerned with the greatest need, God's need. For what is the truth about God's name? Is it anything more than a pious embellishment of reality, a cloak to cover the shame of human evil, an ever weakening tradition, an unintelligible term? When we call upon God, the last thing permitted us is to disregard this need of God's. Rather, we must pray *to* God *on behalf of* God: that he would take up his own cause, that he would assert himself as God, that he would come, that he would appear, that he would reveal himself, that he would arise as God, that he would in very truth become God. This is the deepest source of prayer: God himself compels us to this intercession for God, to this passionate longing that *God will become God.*

For *God's name* is indeed God himself. And *hallowing* is God's own doing. So much his own doing that it is identical with his going into action. "Hallow" is the verb which is derived from God and belongs inseparably to God. For God is the Holy One. "Hallowed be thy name" is as much as to say: Holy One become holy, God become God—in time, in the reality of this world, in history!

All true waiting must resist impatience and endure patiently the tension between having to wait and not being able to wait any longer. So too, waiting on God would not be true waiting if it were not threatened on all sides by the revolt of that impatience which takes the management of God's name into its own hands, or pronounces it to be fraud. Both of these extreme and yet so closely related ways of not letting God be God, that is, of refusing to wait on God, are somehow present in everyone, even in the man who is on the point of waiting on God and repeating after Jesus, "Hallowed be thy name." Our well-established and progressive brethren and those who are still uncertainly seeking are here nearer to each other than they imagine.

For it is true of both that God is not a *possession,* but an *expectation.* But if we are to expect not this or that from God, but first and foremost God himself, then none of us can let God be God without always longing for God to become God for him, to appear to him as God, to answer his seeking, asking, and praying by hallowing His own name. The hallowing of the name is not something additional over and above God's name; it means rather that Gods' name becomes event and thereby God *happens,* God steps out of his anonymity and thus we too are brought out of our anonymity.

That sounds strange to our ears, because we associate *the conception of certain sacred letters* with the name of God, but not the *expectation of the Holy Spirit.* And this in turn goes together with the fact that *words* for us have shriveled to mere *terms,* and that *names* have shrunk to mere *designations.* It is certain that our waiting on God cannot live by terms and designations. For the fact of the matter is, that waiting on God has only the word to hold on to, only the name. For that very reason it remains open to us only to *wait.* But we can also emphasize that for that very reason the waiting *does remain* open to us, even when nothing else remains at all.

For a single word, when it takes place, can lay complete

hold of us and carry us through everything—into the darkness, certainly, yet with the irrefutable expectation that "darkness is not dark to thee." And the name when it is called—called out *over* us so that we are claimed by it, and called upon *by* us so that we lay claim to it—this name when used has the *power* to strike me completely as a person, and gives me the *freedom* completely to respond as a person. Where that happens, there the Holy Spirit is, there God's name is hallowed, there God has become God for us.

But what name of God can do this? It is a strange fact that all the proper names for the gods, including also the proper name of the God of Israel, Yahweh, have faded away before the name of a man of whom I said at the start that he brings us to understand God. Since Jesus' day, all special divine names are over and done with. He who waits on God has now only *one* name he can hold on to: the name of this man Jesus. It is not as if Jesus sought to rob God of his name. On the contrary, Jesus' whole consuming purpose was to announce God in concrete terms and thus to fulfill true waiting on God. He went the whole way *to men,* and this means that in his own person, by his life and finally by his death, as one who waited on God, he set mankind *before God,* and indeed this means that in the true sense of the word he *"presented"* God to mankind in the humanity of God, thereby putting an end to all so-called *ideas* of God.[1]

[1] [This sentence is inevitably somewhat obscure in English. In the German it plays on four different uses and forms of the word *stellen*: the verbs *sich stellen zu* = to go to or join, *stellen vor* = to set before, *vorstellen* = to present or introduce one person to another, and the noun *Vorstellungen* = representations or ideas.—Translator.]

For Jesus not only taught us to pray, "Hallowed be thy name," but, as John's Gospel brings out by way of commentary, Jesus lived this petition, "Father, glorify thy name" (John 12:28). And in the fact that Jesus lived the petition, the glorification or hallowing of God's name was fulfilled. His waiting on God in giving himself for men— or to put it the other way round: *his giving himself for men in waiting on God*—that is *the event of the coming of God.* Thus has God really become God in time, in history, in the reality of this world. God's becoming God takes place as *God's becoming man.*

This has been called the height of paradox. It does in actual fact make no sense when measured by the standards of what man expects from God's becoming God when man projects his own power and glory to infinity, or when he imagines God's becoming God without expecting it. When, however, we pray in Jesus' sense, "Hallowed be thy name," then that God becomes God by becoming man is as clear and self-consistent as a candle that shines and consumes itself in shining. For *humanity*—love to man— is what we can expect from God's *divinity.*

This same fact now meets us again at Christmas in the word of the child in the manger, in a language that is completely simple because completely true. *This is how God hallows his name*—by offering himself to the world in the impotence of a child. God hallows his name in such a way that his love becomes understandable to everyone. All share the same experience: Mary and Joseph, the shepherds and the royal Magi—why, even the animals, ox and ass—have their place in this peace of God's humanity. God hallows his name in such a way that this earthly happening becomes the ground of heavenly jubilation which from that day to this forms part of the accompaniment whenever men pray in Jesus' name: "Our Father, who art in heaven, hallowed be thy name."

But when the golden backdrop of the evangelist Luke's legendary style fades away, then we see all the more clearly that all this means Jesus the *crucified* and that its aim is therefore *faith.* For the faith which is received from this message of Christ is man's participation in God by waiting on him. Faith is therefore *man's becoming man,* or as we are now also, with equal justification and in the same sense, bold to say: *man's becoming God.* For God awaits those who wait on him—he awaits them as his children. It is because we know of Christmas as the fulfillment of the first and greatest petition that our waiting on God has become so full of promise:

> At last you must approval win,
> For you are now of God's own kin,
> For this thank God, ever and aye,
> Content and patient all the day.[2]

[2] [The last verse of Luther's well-known Christmas carol, *Vom Himel kam der Engel Schar,* in *Luther's Works* (Philadelphia: Fortress Press, 1965), Vol. 53, p. 307.—Translator.]

THREE

THY KINGDOM COME

Prayer is turning to God. It is trite to say so, for everyone knows it. To be sure, not everyone does it. We do not find it at all promising. We do not find God at all promising. We expect nothing from him. He seems to be out of date, something that has no future and therefore offers no future either. Hence prayer too appears to be something that has no future and does not in any way alter the future—in other words, pointless. For the future is the whole point of prayer. Prayer is turning to the future.

Perhaps that will make us sit up and take notice, and understand what we are talking about when we speak of prayer. For who would deny that understanding is at least one of the things lacking here, not only among those who do not pray, but also among those who do pray—whether from habit, or constrainedly and convulsively, or in pious self-assurance. Let us take note then that turning to God is to be understood as turning to the future. This goes much deeper than we may at first imagine. If anyone reacts with the feeling that this prejudices his conception of God, and even shakes it violently, then I must reply: surely we all need to be startled out of our sleepy habits and find God to be the most exciting of all words. And there is equal justification for someone to feel that his everyday views of the future are shaken to their foundations when turning to the future is so provocatively equated with turning to God. But that is just what is needed, to combat thoughtlessness in regard to that which gives us most food for thought, namely, the future.

Admittedly, to say that prayer is turning to the future can also appear to be a trite remark. For we know that asking is a particular way of caring [*sorgen,* in the sense of "providing"] for the future. To be sure, we usually get [*besorgen*] our bread at the baker's, but when there is nothing to be had there, because he is out of bread, then the getting [*Besorgen*] of it becomes deep concern about (*Sorge um,* in the sense of "worry about") the future. Then we no doubt understand the petition for our daily bread, although it is precisely in the case of a real emergency that this petition becomes infinitely difficult; nevertheless we usually repeat it easily and cheaply if at all, even though at a well-spread table we still have no less cause to feel the importance of the prayer for our daily bread since it is little enough that separates us from the millions who are starving. But we often do not realize what breathing means until we find ourselves choking and gasping for breath; nor what the future means until we find ourselves in the choking grip of distress, gasping for a future. Each petition of the Our Father is such a cry for a future, a crying out for God's future because there threatens to be no future for man. But in none of the petitions is this cry for a future, for the coming of the conclusive future, the future of all futures, so tersely expressed as in this second one: "Thy kingdom come." Each of the petitions can be understood only as a cry from the depths. This cry for the future of all futures, however, requires as a sort of sounding board the depth of all depths, a participation in the suffering, both guilty and innocent, of all men of all ages.

So this petition should really be quite easy to understand. For we all feel the pressing burden of the fear that ultimately chaos, annihilation, and nothingness will triumph. How could we fail to have sympathy towards the longing for a future of eternal blessedness?

Yet if we are really to understand the degree to which God and the future are one, if we are to be able to pray, "Thy kingdom come," truthfully and not as those who are full of illusions, soberly and not as those who are benumbed by wishful thinking and childish ideas, then it is necessary to say something which appears to run counter to all we have said so far and even to contradict our text. Perhaps only a startling objection will make us take notice.

Why still keep praying for the *coming* of God's kingdom, when surely it *is here,* in our midst? Turning to the future in the expectation that it will bring the kingdom of God could actually be the expression of turning against God—a flight from the sovereignty of God through a desire for self-assertion. As long as I understand the kingdom of God to be a welcome continuation of this life and this world beyond the point at which they come to an end, at all events in their present form; as long as the infinite continuation of time—my time!—is what I mean by the future with which the second petition deals; as long as I confuse the kingdom of God itself with my conception of its *results;* and as long as *changed conditions* and God's sovereignty over *others* seem to me more important than his rule over *myself*—then this prayer for the coming of God's kingdom is blasphemy. We shall learn properly to pray, "Thy kingdom come," only when we strictly forbid ourselves all dreams about the future, only when we summarily dismiss from our minds all ideas of having to wait, or being permitted to wait, for some more or less distant day, for a new era of history, or for what comes after this temporal life, and instead of all that utter our confessing, thankful, adoring Amen to the kingdom of God which *has come.*

This should be no surprise to those who know Jesus. I should be making myself the enemy of Jesus and pronouncing him a fool, if in the face of his preaching and his life I were to deny that here the sovereignty of God has broken in. There can be no more waiting for another event, a higher revelation, a more convincing demonstration of power, a greater gift. If we do not recognize that to participate in what Jesus has given is to participate in the kingdom of God, if we do not allow the sovereignty of God to act upon ourselves through the faith-creating word, then our understanding of the second petition must be perverted in a sense contrary to Jesus and our prayer for the coming of God's kingdom must be lacking all power.

This point holds for our treatment of the whole of the Lord's Prayer, and indeed for all our praying. Each petition must be prayed as a petition already fulfilled, as unwaveringly certain of what has already been given, as a prayer that has its ground in gratitude, and now asks for the abiding continuance of what has already begun. If we say "kingdom of God" and think of something still outstanding, of all the signs of its failure and its absence, and then set our hopes on tumultuous acts of divine power fashioned like acts of human power which are projected to infinity— if we do all that instead of making room for the righteousness, the peace, and the joy which come to us from and in the name of Jesus and indeed are even held out to us imploringly as though man had no need to ask but God were rather the suppliant of man: "Be reconciled to God" (II Cor. 5:20)—then, without such a change in our understanding of the second petition, we do not pray in the name and the power of Jesus.

For to pray in the name of Jesus for the coming of God's kingdom is to pray not for the absent but for the present kingdom of God, not for a kingdom whose time is not yet come, but for the kingdom whose time was long ago proclaimed and, if we would only listen, is proclaimed in every sermon and every testimony to Jesus Christ: "Behold, now is the acceptable time; behold, now is the day of salvation" (II Cor. 6:2). This is a kingdom for whose coming we can pray calmly and confidently because it is one that has already come and is constantly coming. "Thy kingdom come"—that, if we would only understand it aright, is nothing other than wondering assent to what is happening, to what is actually coming.

It might therefore be helpful if for once—as a sort of exercise—we were to drop the expression "kingdom of God." Much use, and much more misuse, has worn it thin, to say nothing of the fact that we ourselves have grown so accustomed to it that we have become dead of all feeling for it. We must still rediscover this word, and what comes to us in it. We said a moment ago that the time of the kingdom of God was proclaimed long ago and is constantly being proclaimed—for precisely that is the point of Christian proclamation. It may be helpful now to say "time of God" instead of "kingdom of God." The "kingdom of God" we usually almost inevitably conceive of as a state or condition. The tendency to *form conceptions* of what has to do with God all too easily corrupts the things of faith into words of unbelief. The idea that the kingdom of God is a state inevitably corrupts the present kingdom of God into becoming the absent kingdom of God. So let us for once say "time of God" instead of "kingdom of God"! It may sound ironical when I seek to justify the demand for this linguistic exercise by emphasizing that the helpful thing about the phrase "time of God" is that it is difficult to form any conception of it. What I mean is this: we are thereby cut off from taking refuge in our conceptions of the kingdom of God, and this also puts an end to the ready excuses we offer for evading the message of the kingdom of God altogether: "I cannot conceive of that!" We are not asked to conceive of anything at all. We are rather asked to *hear* what time it is, what hour has struck.

Now it would be very tempting indeed to announce the time after the fashion of apocalyptic revival sermons by proclaiming threateningly that it is five minutes to zero hour. What, however, have gone by the board as old apocalyptic ideas are then usually replaced by modern features, such as the menace of atomic death. No doubt there is also an element of truth in this way of announcing the time—incidentally, all too much truth to allow the normal

preacher in the pulpit to be equal to what he is really letting himself in for in such attempts to give relevance to his otherwise, as he thinks, irrelevant message. It is not at all a good thing to exploit the justified fears of mankind in order to restore a more interesting note to preaching that has otherwise become dull and meaningless, and thus to see our essential preaching task as proclaiming the fact that it is five minutes to zero hour. No doubt that too has its place in Christian proclamation, but it is not the essential thing, not the decisive thing. The essential thing, the decisive thing, the thing that makes Christian proclamation so unspeakably glorious, is that in the name of Jesus we are to proclaim the time of God: "Now is the acceptable time, now is the day of salvation," as Paul puts it. And that most certainly means that now in the midst of the atomic age, now in the midst of the time of the super powers of East and West, God's time is come, God has his time, God draws us into his time. I wish to make three further points about this way of announcing the time.

First, this way of announcing the time joins together what man has put asunder, namely, God and time. That sounds offensive, and precisely the opposite sounds so pious, namely, putting God as the Eternal beyond time, and keeping time as the limited, earthly, human, well clear of God. But with this kind of piety we make God unreal and reality godless, and thus we lose both God and reality. To be sure, God is the Eternal. Yet eternity is not the prolongation of time; it is rather the true fulfillment of time. That is why the Johannine Christ says: "This is eternal life, that they know thee the only true God, and Jesus Christ whom thou hast sent (John 17:3). "He who

has the Son has life" (I John 5:12). Time which is fulfilled is the time which God bestows on us. Not, however, in the wretched sense of a time that is separated from God, empty of God; rather, in the sense that God bestows time on us by having time for us, making time for us, drawing us out of our own time that has been perverted to a godless thing and into his time that is determined by him. Thus we too have time for God and allow our time to be determined by him; we are there for God because God is there for us. This is God's kingdom, the sovereignty of God, not beyond, but in the time which God by his coming has made his own.

Secondly, this way of announcing the time makes our time controversial. It is crude to hold that time is unequivocal and to imagine that time as told by the clock is the true essence of time. The true measure of time is not the clock. The true measure of time—this sounds strange, but is worth thinking about—is hope. What makes time controversial is the question whether it is time that is empty, hopeless, void of future, or whether it is time that is fulfilled, hopeful, loaded to the brim, so to speak, with future. It was to kindle this very controversy of time that Jesus came. Here is the meaning of such words as: "I came to cast fire upon the earth; and would that it were already kindled! . . . Do you think that I have come to give peace on earth? No, I tell you, but rather division" (Luke 12:49, 51).

We have not understood what the kingdom of God is all about as long as we have not yet been drawn into the conflict between the kingdom of God and the kingdom of a world which refuses to be God's creation any longer. In

precisely the same way, we have not understood what the time of God means so long as we do not find ourselves involved in the controversial character of time. As the old man, the sinful man, I belong to the time that is empty, vain, lost, hopeless, void of future. As the new man, the man of faith, I belong to the time that is filled with eternity, determined by God, hopeful, rewarding, laden with future. The old man is called "old" for the very reason that he is antiquated, subject to the past. His humanity is a hopeless thing without any future, no matter how many illusions he himself erects concerning the future and no matter how much he longs for the time to pass for the sake of the allegedly better days of which he dreams. For to long for the time to pass is a sign that we are subject to a meaningless time and do not live in God's time. The new man on the other hand is called "new," because he is one who looks to God and thus to the future. That, however, does not mean a future for the sake of which he wishes the time would pass, so as to become like the devil, one who has no time; he rather looks to a future which fulfills the present and allows man to live wholly in the present as one who, like God, has time. We may allow this to correct what we have said about the true measure of time, not in order to retract our statement, but only to protect it against misunderstanding. We said that the true measure of time is hope. We have understood that correctly only when we can also say that the true measure of time is love. For love has time, and makes time, and bestows time. Love is the essence of God's time. Love is the fullness of the sovereignty of God.

And thirdly, this way of announcing the time encourages us to pray for the coming of the kingdom of God. We are not now contradicting the fact that the kingdom of God is here, in our midst. It is present only in that it comes. It is present only in that it is announced, proclaimed, and hailed by our thus announcing the time of God. Thus the proclamation of Jesus Christ is the kingdom of God in action. And participation in the kingdom of God takes place only through the faith which works love; but because this participation is through faith, it therefore is constantly asking and constantly receiving, and hence constantly giving thanks. For God, who comes to us only in the word that works faith, is essentially the Coming One. To have God means to let God come. Faith is letting God come. Believing means receiving God. That is the true meaning of the words which Luke puts on Mary's lips: "Behold I am the handmaid of the Lord; let it be to me according to your word" (Luke 1:38). Faith as the receiving of God therefore never ceases to pray, "Thy kingdom come." We pray it as long as God grants us time. We pray it in the certainty that when our time is done God will "wipe away every tear from their eyes, and death shall be no more, neither shall there be mourning nor crying nor pain any more . . ." For God is "the Alpha and the Omega, the beginning and the ending, who is, and who was, and who is to come, the Almighty" (Rev. 21:4, 6; 1:8).

FOUR

THY WILL BE DONE,
ON EARTH AS IT IS IN HEAVEN

"Heaven and earth"—that, in the language of the Bible, is the world. "Thy will be done in the world." So Jesus taught us to speak and to pray. So we are to repeat after him in our speaking and praying. Admittedly, "repeat after" has an odious sound. An idea of thoughtlessness and lack of independence has become associated with this particular expression of piety, and unfortunately not without reason. In actual fact, however, prayer is not praying without thinking. So we are now invited to think about what we have already all too often repeated without thought, so that in truly repeating the prayer after Jesus we may entrust ourselves to this word of assurance and commit our lives to it in its movement towards freedom: "Thy will be done in the world."

The fact that prayer reminds us of the world should give us food for thought right at the start. Usually prayer is considered to be turning one's back on the world. To be sure, prayer does involve collecting our thoughts, withdrawing from things, and desisting from activities in order to submit to the call to be still. But the fact that some have great difficulty or do not succeed at all in this, may ultimately have the same ground as causes others to construct a technique of religious withdrawal which has the insipid flavor of something not convincingly necessary and out of touch with real life. Both the atrophy of prayer and these special techniques of prayer are the result of halfheartedness—that split thinking which tries to do justice to God and the world apart from each other, fifty-fifty, or usually in a less balanced proportion.

But what if God, to whom we turn when we turn our back on the world, himself has his face rather than his back to the world? Then prayer either becomes an attempt to reshape God according to our own will, thus becoming idolatry—there is also a Christian variety of that—or else it turns to face the world with God. It is with this turning to face the world with God that the third petition of the Our Father is concerned. Perhaps our praying, insofar as we do pray at all seriously, is such a lame business and such a forced affair, rather than an act of assurance and an act of freedom, precisely because it does not turn to face the world as God does. Thus praying shows itself to be only a semblance of turning to God. Such pretended turning to God, however, is in reality merely a withdrawal into a religious corner of the world and an enduring entanglement in a false worldliness.

Prayer is not a matter of pleasant contemplation. To pray—and by that I do not mean merely an isolated religious act, but, more comprehensively, every serious use of the name of God, every act of appealing to him, of speaking of him, of thinking about him, since it is prayer that first makes plain what it means to say "God"—to pray, then, is to submit oneself, so it seems, to a durability test. On the one hand we lay hold of God and on the other hand we have the world. That is of course inconceivable, for the two cannot be set side by side, and yet anyone who attempts it can experience at least from a distance the counterpull of two infinite forces. It is not a case here of that lamentable division we know only too well. We say, "Hallowed be thy name"—and are concerned about our own good name! We say, "Thy kingdom come"—but with the mental reservation, "only not too soon!" We say, "Thy will be done"—but "I hope I shall be lucky!" The only real answer to this is: don't cling so fast to your little bit of world! Let go, and stop standing in the way of your own prayer! What we are speaking of here, however, is the act of turning towards the world as God does—learning to say God and world in one breath, to hold them together in a single sentence. The cross has become, as it were, the shorthand sign for such nearness between God and the world: "God so loved the world . . ." But the cross is no mere symbol; it reminds us of a specific event, and as a memory it again becomes a specific event. For faith stands with Jesus between God and the world. Stands? No—faith lives as surrender to the God-world-event.

That sounds strange, and yet it is only compressing the sentence, "Thy will be done, on earth as it is in heaven," into a single expression: God-world-event. We are all of us involved in this event, whether we like it or not. And according to temperament and experience we may give very different descriptions of our place in this event: as ceaseless work or pleasant drifting, as repeatedly "coming off all right" or as being buffeted, bruised, and broken.

But it is one thing merely to be objectively involved in what happens here, and quite another thing to be in it in such a way that we risk the responsibility of answering for it as God-world-event.

That too sounds surprising. Who can answer for world events? And should we expect this to be possible when we proceed to set them in such peculiar conjunction with God as God-world-events? It is quite true that no one can answer for world events as such. But to speak of God with our eye on these world events is surely nothing other than to answer for them—not treating them with thoughtless indifference, not speaking irresponsibly of them, yet not holding our peace either, in resignation or dismay. This is to stand by these world events in word, not as outside commentators; no, as men who are ourselves involved, and at the same time as men who by our words exercise an influence on the events. "Thy will be done in the world." Does that not confirm that praying is a test of durability, interposing us between the counterpull of two infinite forces?

World events and the will of God—who can reconcile the two, even if only in breathing a sigh in which there is still at least a glimmer of hope. We are reminded of the Crucified. How far does he encourage us to pray, "Thy will be done in the world"? In Luke's shorter form of the Lord's Prayer this petition is missing. Perhaps that is in fact, historically speaking, the more original version. But it does not in the least alter the close relation between Jesus and this petition. The same evangelist, indeed, sets the coming of Jesus—in the prayer of Mary—and the departure of Jesus—in the prayer in Gethsemane—in the light of this petition: "Thy will be done." Yet before Jesus can give us courage to pray this, we must be ready to receive from him our first lessons in understanding this petition.

For on this petition there prevails an extraordinary degree of confusion. None of the petitions of the Lord's Prayer is, so to speak, of peculiarly Christian origin. None guarantees by its wording that it will be understood in terms of faith. Wherever men pray, we find distant or even near echoes. This need not cause us any uncertainty in regard to the prayer of our Lord. On the contrary, it shows how completely the whole human race in all its need, in all its distress and longing, is here drawn up into the simplest of words and now must also be drawn out of the tangle of misunderstanding into the simple truth. It is no wonder that the confusion is especially great when we come to speak of world events. For here all are involved, whether on a narrower or a wider scale—Christians, Jews, and Gentiles—and not only the religious, but also the godless and the supposedly neutral.

The world is of course not a stationary object, but pure event through and through. Where and how the world actually concerns man, is not a question of automatic processes, but of *acts of will*. This is no mere theory, but solely the indisputable experience which every man has of himself and of his fellow men; here is a wild sea of willing and being unwilling, of good will and ill will, of strength of will and weakness of will. And within and beyond that sea is the strange wake of enticements and restrictions, favorable and unfavorable forces, powers of resistance, and over all the enigma of destiny. Some give it a name, others leave it impersonal and anonymous; and yet none can evade the question of meaning. But where there is meaning, there is will—even if it is explained as senseless caprice.

To say "God," is to relate world events to the will of God. But how? Not only between world views, religions, and theologies is this point in dispute, but everyone joins in, in his everyday conversation and life, and above all in his conscience. For that is where the decision is made about his will, and about what he thinks of the God-world-events and where he takes his stand in them.

Those who are no longer at home with talk of God can regard the petition, "Thy will be done in the world," only as a piece of inconsistent nonsense. For either God's will is not done, and then he is not God and prayer is senseless; or else world events are after all the doing of God's will, and then there is no need for prayer, and God, moreover, is then not God either. For how could he who wills the events of the world as they are, without exception and without gloss, be God? Such captious arguments may perhaps not impress us. Behind them, however, can lie abysmal experiences which, because we have been spared, probably do not impress us. Let us beware of judging! And let us realize how near we are to those who have no inkling of God, and how deeply we share their guilt!

The religious fanatic, in the long run, also does away with the petition, "Thy will be done in the world." He makes it a battle cry. He imagines himself to know God's will and commands; and now it only remains for him to put them into practice and transform the world accordingly. Such fanatical activism could very well be awak-

ened by the drowsiness of Christians and the gratified sat-
isfaction of our congregations which are like veterans'
organizations which spend their time cultivating their traditions, acting like anything but a body of active troops.
And it is certainly essential to do God's will. Yet God's
will not only stretches infinitely beyond anything we do;
it also never allows itself to be usurped by our will, and
constantly remains effective, self-active will. Thus only
prayer can ultimately accord with the will of God.

The legalist makes well-being the measure of God's will
in world events. He is the representative of the kind of
piety which seems to come naturally to man, whether he
be strait-laced or lax, or at all events he is the pagan
whose rumblings can be heard in us all, even Christians.
God's gracious will is that which answers to our own
wishes. God's wrath is that which interferes with our happiness. The legalist knows of course that sometimes he too
deserves to be punished, but he also knows which events
are to be regarded as punishment, which as forbearance,
and which as reward and blessing. Thus his own small
scale experience and the large scale events of the world are
given religious evaluations. And since the account never
quite balances, the final settlement is then left to the beyond, and thus the unhappiness that cannot be accounted
for is ultimately also borne patiently as the will of God.
This provides a whole medley of possible ways of praying,
"Thy will be done." They often look deceptively like faith,
but it is not the eye that is here called to judge. To be
sure, the distinction between true faith and paganism in
Christian dress is outwardly voiced in our preaching, but
it is in the hiddenmost places of the heart that the deci-

sion between them is made. We Christians can barely sense the depths to which our piety is rooted in the pagan equation of God's will and our wishes, and how urgently necessary it therefore is for all of us together, ministers and congregations, to take preaching more seriously, so that we might learn and practice what is really meant by faith in the Crucified One as the essence of the Gospel.

Finally, philosophers have derived from the heritage of dying religions the idea that all that happens in the world is the incomprehensible will of the deity to which the wise man bows in order to be in harmony with his destiny. This can sometimes be most touchingly expressed and can look deceptively like the attitude of "Not as I will, but as thou wilt." Should not we Christians of all people take notice when acquiescence, submissiveness, and contentment are not only taught but also lived? But is that the meaning of our prayer: "Thy will be done in the world"? Certainly it is usually understood as submitting to the mysterious will of God. But this is not at all what Jesus had in mind. Thus understood it would not be a prayer of faith, and not a word of assurance or a move towards freedom.

For the understanding necessary to give us courage to pray this petition, it is well to return once more to the exact wording, "Thy will be done, on earth as it is in heaven." For "heaven and earth" we have put "world." And that is still true. And yet we must now give heed to the note we have so far completely passed over: the world stands in contradiction to itself, because it finds itself at war with God. For on the one hand it is in very truth God's world where God's will is done without opposition and God is given the glory—the place where his splendor,

78

his peace, his joy dwell. On the other hand it is the perverted, godless world, albeit the world that is never sev-
ered from God but is delivered over to the hidden, absent
God.

Men of old conceived of this in terms of two spheres.
To us that appears naïve, now that man, with his searching
mind and with such a fullness of technical power, has pen-
etrated into the world of space. Yet even though it is
true that the ancients had, scientifically speaking, a naïve
picture of the world, the way in which they experienced
reality was far from naïve. It is we who are naïve when
we imagine that our scientific knowledge has settled once
and for all their talk of heaven and earth.

For it is simply true—and this neither naïve conceptions
nor naïve criticisms must be allowed to hide from us—that
where we men pursue the way of our own will in accord
with our own will, there—palpably or secretly—is a deep
ill will towards God. That is why God is to us the distant,
the hidden. It is quite true to say that God is not "there,"
as objects are "there"; we cannot reckon with him as we
are accustomed to reckon with things. And therefore the
world too, as the place of his revealed presence, is deeply
hidden from us, or, as we say, does not "exist": it is conceivable only as the absolutely transcendent and future,
and hence not "conceivable" at all. To us the world is
still—and more than ever so today—this divided world.
On the one hand the world is revealed to us as the place
in which our will, though not by any means unbrokenly,
rules or at least seeks to rule, the world in which God has
no place and in which his will manifestly is not done. On
the other hand the world is completely hidden from us,

and as far as it is concerned our will is as impotent as our understanding is blind; it is the world in which God's majesty is revealed and everything goes according to his will.

And now in the teeth of this division in the world we are encouraged to pray, "Thy will be done, on earth as it is in heaven." This surely means: may heaven come upon earth and the earth become heaven. May the realm of ill will against God be broken, and the will of God be manifestly done in us, and by us, and around us. Is that the spirit of submissiveness? Is it not a spirit of revolution in comparison with which what we know as the revolutionary spirit becomes the most harmless romanticism? Jesus teaches no submission to world events. For how could one declare war on what we call world events in sharper terms than by saying, here on earth God's will is to be done as manifestly and unopposedly as it is in heaven? If that were really to happen, then not merely this or that but everything would be different. So here is no submission to the unalterable course of world events, but—and this is a very different thing—submission to the will of God in the form of a surrender to the revealing, the coming, the coming about of God's will. For the will of God, as it is here appealed to and proclaimed, invoked, even implored, is not identical to the world events that are before our eyes; it is actually a counterevent opposed to these world events.

But is this not pure visionariness? If not in the sense of fanatical activism, then at least an excess of religious fantasy bereft of all ground in reality? It certainly threatens to be so if in our treatment of this petition we do not keep fast our bearings by three orientation points which are like the stars that enable us to hold our course by night on the open sea.

The first is: without question *everything that happens is an event of God's will.* If we do not hold to this, then we do become visionaries. But any event of the will of God is to us totally hidden and inscrutable. Even in all the ill will towards God, God's will is also at work. And so too, for example, the starving and dying of millions is the dark, inscrutable will of God, just as our participation in commercial prosperity with all its pleasant and happy consequences is nothing else but the dark, inscrutable will of God. If we do not risk the confession that all that happens, happens according to God's hidden will, and if we are not able to subject that confession to the unreserved testing of our experience of the world, we ought not to speak of God. So is it after all a case of blind submission to the obscure will of God? Provided we know what we are saying when we describe this as God's will, the word "submission" would be quite proper. But precisely in order to know this a second point is required.

This second point of orientation is: *the revealed will of God takes place as clear, luminous word.* God's law is certainly included here: what we men are told, what we are to do, what the Lord demands of us, and what, even when we fail, remains not only true but also operative as the inescapable discipline of the law that constrains and compels even the rebellious. But the will of God in the form of the law is only the shadow of his revealed will. For the latter is the Gospel, which shines so full of Advent promise in our petition, when understood aright: "On earth as it is in heaven." It is God's revealed will that the world

81

become one by becoming one with him, that the world be reconciled to God and so also be reconciled in itself. This revealed will is on the way, it is already being done, has already been done, and intends to be further done as the still outstanding end and goal of the will of the hidden God. This is the real aim of this petition, "Thy will be done, on earth as it is in heaven." This surely means: may Jesus Christ, the mediator between God and man, the reconciler of the world—may he be done, i.e., may he be proclaimed and believed, may he rule through his word in faith.

And the third point of orientation is: thus we *can face the events of the world in the freedom which grows out of assurance.* We know where we belong, we know what counts, we know what has a future. In this liberating assurance we make room in the world for God's will—the will with which God loves the world. We make room for it in prayer. Then through our life too the revealed will of God begins to be done—the shining of true love to the world.

FIVE

GIVE US THIS DAY
OUR DAILY BREAD

This clause in the middle of the Lord's Prayer does not seem to measure up to the heights to which our eyes are raised by the first three petitions—God's name, God's kingdom, God's will; and just as little is it a match for the depths that open in the following three petitions—our debts, our temptations, our lostness. The prayer for our daily bread stands unpretentiously in between, with its face towards natural, everyday, matter-of-fact things. What concerns us here seems scarcely worth speaking of, compared with the infinite significance of the other things that are expressed in the Our Father. On the one hand we have the things of God, which can be summed up in one comprehensive term, his word; on the other hand we have the things of us men, which in face of God means, in a nutshell, our failure. Surely these two elements are the real governing factors in prayer. God's word is the epitome of all that allows us to pray and gives us courage to do so. Our failure is the epitome of all that makes prayer necessary and drives us to it—perhaps this failure also hinders us in it, but at all events it marks the place where prayer as a cry from the depths takes place with ultimate seriousness and overwhelming necessity.

How do we fit the solid, material bread intended for our mouths and stomachs into this spiritual transaction between God and man? What right do we have still to assert an interest in the preservation and needs of our earthly life, when we should be concerned about the claim of the righteousness of God upon us and when everything which we hold grave and important is put into the shadows by the question of our justification before God? Between the eternal God and our ultimate future—whether it be eternal death or eternal life—what room is there for this almost niggardly attention to the fleeting, insignificant things of today? And still more surprisingly, what room is there for the paltry daily ration that is needed in order to eke out our life from today till tomorrow? Many a pious man has felt embarrassed at the presence of such a trivial matter in the middle of the Lord's Prayer, and has therefore interpreted daily bread only in spiritual terms. But even when taken literally, this petition is regarded as the humblest and least of them all, and one that in contrast to its extraordinarily central place really belongs to the outer margin of the Lord's Prayer. Normally, it even appears to be superfluous, since our bread—and much more than bread—is in plentiful supply, and the petitioner is himself responsible for earning and providing his own.

Yet all such reflections to the contrary, it is no accident that this unpretentious clause stands in the center. It is in fact the very heart of the Lord's Prayer. Let this not unleash a foolish argument about the order of priority among the individual petitions. They are one. None competes with the others. Each calls for the others. And each contains the whole. This is also true of the petition for

our daily bread, though here most hiddenly. But it is precisely in the task of grasping even here the hidden presence of the whole prayer that this petition becomes the heart of the Lord's Prayer.

The point of each petition is to unite God and man. What Jesus truly is, according to the fundamental Christian confession—the union of God and man, true God and true man—that we spell out after him, as it were, in the prayer which he taught us. Even the invocation, "Our Father," takes this fundamental theme of the uniting of God and man and sets it fairly and squarely in the foreground. What is the aim of the first petitions with their constant "Thy, thy, thy," save that our opposition to God be broken and we men be brought into unity with God— with his name, his kingdom, his will? What is the point of the other petitions, which deal so emphatically with our side, save that we be thrown not upon our own resources and left to ourselves, but that God should take care of us—our debts, our failure, our lostness—in such a way that all is taken from us and up into his grace?

The prayer for daily bread also strikes the dominant note of bringing God and man together—and it does it at the very point at which even the thought of God is usually most removed from our minds: in the natural, everyday, matter-of-fact world, where we are concerned with satisfying our bodily needs, where our interest turns to food, where our attention is completely taken up by the struggle for existence, where we are committed to immediate, tangible things, things that are fleeting and yet at this juncture highly important, the things of today, the demands of the moment.

There is in fact a certain propriety in our distance from God, and even in our apparent lack of any relation to God, in this realm of the profane and the completely human. We cannot and must not try to substitute the care of the soul for the care of the body. To give to the hungry pious phrases instead of bread can be worse than giving them stones. Man's own tasks and responsibilities are not to be foisted onto God. No amount of praying exonerates man from his work in the kitchen, in the workshop, at the steering wheel, at the desk, or wherever in the widest sense of the term he has to earn his daily bread. Eternity does not make time a matter of indifference, and thinking of the future end does not by any means cancel the provisional demands of today and tomorrow.

This sobering and stringent view of the earthly, temporal realities must not on any account be toned down by flowery religious phrases which make only a semblance of bringing God and this reality of ours together and do not take either with real seriousness. To be sure, we are hardly in any danger of casting a legalistic network of religious rules over the whole of life in order to regulate the foods which are clean and unclean, allowed and forbidden, or the times and places which are sacred and profane. But even those elements of religious custom and experience alive among us move us to ask whether God and our everyday realities are so genuinely and closely related to each other as the petition for daily bread implies. For either the two simply go side by side, interest in bread and interest in God, or thoughts of prayer and thanks to God are merely a decorative descant accompanying the really dominant thing, the so-called "real" life which in fact remains

untouched by them. But can it really be such a harmless affair when God and man meet, not merely at occasional highpoints in life and not merely in the catastrophic depths of our existence, but in the matter-of-fact things of everyday?

Really, though, is anything still matter-of-fact when we are expected to think of God and man as so closely united that even bread, that epitome of the corporeal and commonplace character of human life, is to be thought of at the same time as God, and God at the same time as bread? Such thinking in fact puts an end to that deceptive matter-of-factness which prevents us from noticing, hearing, and understanding what everyday things are saying to us. That the things with which we deal have turned dumb and have nothing to say to us, that they have consequently lost their living coherence and become dead objects is a symptom—and certainly not an insignificant one—of our foolishness, our thoughtlessness, our hardheartedness. The result is that we ourselves become increasingly dumb without having anything to say—or it may be, loquacious, also without really having anything to say. The more awake, attentive, and open our hearts become, the more meaningful and eloquent everything around us becomes and the more everything joins together in a single, living coherence. Bread is then no longer merely a thing to be regarded in physical or chemical terms, no longer merely a means of nourishment or of enjoyment, but it is eloquent bread, bearing, so to speak, words that concern us. And this is not because it has a voice of its own, as is found in fairy tales, but because God's word is present in all that is.

When faith confesses that all that is, is created by God's

word, then it is also saying that God's word clings to all that is. Our ears are not so live, our hearts not so pure, that we can hear and understand God's word in all that encounters us. But if the claim that God speaks in our proclamation is no empty claim, but one faithful to its own promise, then we will see it in the fact that through the word of proclamation the things around us will acquire more of their word character, fulfilling once again what according to God's will they were meant to be and to say. And thus it is a fruit of proclamation when all separated, mutually isolated, torn, and disrupted elements in our lives once again come together, since by God's will they belong together.

We have said that the point of prayer is the uniting of God and man. Thus in prayer all the things that belong to our life, including also the most natural, commonplace, matter-of-fact things, come into contact with the word, and indeed themselves become word. For God and man are united through the word. And where God is with man and man with God, there the word of God rules and reality is transformed by the word. There bread too is transformed, not into something alien or different, but into what it really is. It is transformed from an alienated, outward thing that says nothing to us, into bread that is given by God, from godless bread to bread for which we have to thank God. The ultimate aim of the prayer for daily bread is not that we should receive bread as such, but that we should receive it for what it is—as God's bread, in which and with which is God's word.

What is the tenor of this word which belongs to bread? First of all it impresses on us quite simply our *dependence on bread.* The first thing to be said of man before God is that like all living things he is, so to speak, a hungering being. Living and being in need are one and the same thing. We are in a bad way when we cannot satisfy our hunger. But we are in an equally bad way when we no longer feel any hunger.

This most vital need of man for food binds him very closely to time. The stomach demands its daily rights. Even all of man's great achievements by which human power and riches are unfolded in the economic and technical world, in civilization and culture, have behind them the active urges that spring from man's indigence. However high he climbs in the spiritual world, man remains dependent on the material nurture of his body. However much he may boast of his independence, man can exist at all only through this constant supply of strength from without.

There is no reason to be ashamed of this or to strive against it, as if it were pious to seek liberation from our earthly needs and to struggle desperately towards that end. Nor would it be proper to regard this aspect of human existence as something that is of no consequence in God's eyes. On the contrary man, precisely in the lifting up of his heart to God in prayer, ought to be aware of what he is in his creatureliness, his frailty, his transience, his dependence on such trifles as a piece of bread, a handful of rice, a cup of water. He may be used to more and better than this bare minimum of existence. But when he appears before God, he should remember this minimum of existence, and let himself be brought down from his pedestal to recognize the slender thread by which his life hangs.

The word that belongs to bread impresses on us, further, our *dependence on our fellow men.* To be sure, it reminds us of our duty to see to our own upkeep as soon as we are able and as long as we are able, and not to become an unnecessary burden to our fellow men. It is in the Bible, and not by any means first in the manifesto of a socialist party, that we find the stringent word: "If any one will not work, let him not eat" (II Thess. 3:10). There was a time when begging was held up as a sign of sanctity. We have no wish to pass judgment on that. Even today, the praise of poverty could acquire a new meaning for us as a protest against the effects of commercial boom and economic miracle. There is profound truth in the insight that man is at bottom a beggar—in every role he plays on earth. The last words Luther wrote on a scrap of paper before his death were: "We are beggars, that is true." He knew that, not because he had once belonged to a mendicant order, but because he had been stripped of even that halo.

But there is also a less profound sense in which, in spite of our own labor and our own earnings, we are reminded by our daily bread and all that belongs to it of our dependence on our fellow men. We do not need to think of the highly complicated structures of modern economics at all in order to realize the extent of our dependence upon factors of social life. Even in the narrowest circles of our lives we experience this in manifold ways, provided that we have not become altogether obtuse towards what seems to be a matter of course. This dependence on our fellow men is not merely, or even first and foremost, a burden. It is a blessing which we are mostly not aware of until no one takes any interest in us and we have to eat our bread day in and day out alone.

There is profound significance in the fact that eating is an act of fellowship, not because this is the more rational way, but because it is through our daily bread, through our dependence on it, through receiving and enjoying and handing it to each other, that fellowship is supremely constituted. Jesus received sinners by eating with them. The Gospels are full of this relationship between the bread by which we live and the fellowship in which we live. Even the fellowship of heaven is presented as a banquet.

Therefore it is a matter of course that our petition runs: "Give *us* this day *our* daily bread." Just as it would be impossible to alter this petition by the inclusion of more ambitious wishes regarding food, so it would be impossible to reduce it to individualistic terms. One cannot before God pray for bread for oneself alone. The bracketing together of our relation to God and our relation to our neighbor, as expressed in the next petition, "Forgive us our debts, as we also have forgiven our debtors," is surely also valid here: give us this day our daily bread, as we give it this day to those who ask us for it. Must not the petition, when so expounded, die on our lips? How deaf we are to this word that belongs to our daily bread—this word by which we ourselves are summoned to the giving of bread! The "Bread for the World" collection, as we are proudly told, has achieved a higher total than was expected. But let us be sober in our judgment: when all is said and done, what shamefully paltry alms we give—a crust that we give away, because we are already stuffed! And what cunning stratagems have to be used to elicit even that little! The fact that millions today are starving apparently does not yet speak plainly enough; it is not of itself enough to move our sluggish hearts. The proximity of the prayer for our daily bread and the prayer for the forgiveness of our debts is in very truth so close that both have to be said in one breath.

This gives peculiar weight to our last and decisive point: the word that belongs to our bread reveals to us our *dependence on God*. It is true that the idea of daily bread points us precisely to that wide realm of life that is left to the activity of man. By the will of God it is man's business to see to the matter of daily bread, and therefore also to bear responsibility for the hungry. The prayer for daily bread does not by any means afford an easy way to the goal, or a supplementary guarantee. It would be completely misunderstood if regarded as a prayer only for emergencies, so that we could quite well and quite happily spare ourselves the trouble of praying it today. It is necessary at all times, in abundance as in hunger. For our part in the business of daily bread, our possibilities and therefore also duties, can be rightly grasped, understood, and put into practice only when we know how to distinguish them from God's part in the business and from what he alone can do. The power of man is indeed great, but to a certain extent it hangs by the thread of man's impotence. We do not need to refer to the monsters which our age supplies by way of illustration. The humblest of everyday experiences teaches that all our doings are subject to the inescapable condition: if God wills and we are spared. The Psalmist's word is simple and true: "It is in vain that you rise up early, to go late to rest, eating the bread of anxious toil; for he gives to his beloved in sleep" (Psalm 127:2).

Yet there is not one single chain of cause and effect running from our dependence on bread to our dependence on God. The word which reveals our dependence on God becomes the very contradiction of our dependence on bread. Dependence on God is rightly understood only when it becomes the ground of our freedom. To take everyday things into our prayer means to make our dependence on God the means of raising our everyday dependencies into the sphere of freedom. The everyday dependencies are not thereby set aside, but are put to their right use. Only the man whose dependence on God has liberated him to live in freedom has no need to let himself become enslaved to his earthly dependencies, and yet is free to assent to them.

This would have to be transposed into as many keys as there is richness and variety in life: this God-given freedom *from* our daily bread and freedom *for* our daily bread, and likewise, when rightly understood, the God-given freedom *from* our fellow man and freedom *for* our fellow man, the God-given freedom *from* today and freedom *for* today. Precisely in these everyday relationships in which every man stands does the word of God take concrete shape: faith takes concrete shape in our dealings with bread and all that belongs to it, love in our dealings with our fellow men, hope in our dealings with time, with the step from today to tomorrow. If only we would recognize how the union of God and man, the incarnation of God in Jesus and the divine sonship of man made possible through him, has its goal in the things of everyday—and how everyday things before God belong to the heart of prayer!

SIX

FORGIVE US OUR DEBTS,
AS WE ALSO HAVE FORGIVEN OUR DEBTORS

That necessity teaches prayer, is a dubious assertion. Nevertheless, there is no doubt that praying allows us to dwell only on what is necessary. Thus it is distinguished from wishing.

Wishing is playing with possibilities. Of this we have ample experience. With a hundred francs in our pocket we can dream of the fulfillment of many wishes at that price, but only one of them can be realized. Most of our wishes remain in the realm of fantasy. And this is generally a good thing. Nevertheless, wishing has its proper place. It is a sign of liveliness. The man who sheds his wishes as a tree in autumn sheds its leaves, shows that his soul is weary and dying. This is not, however, to be mistaken for dying in the spirit which by no means makes the believer look dried-up and barren in this life. Prayer does not kill our wishing, but purifies it and points to its limits. In this way our wishes also have a place in our prayer, like all other creaturely things. Not that they may dominate, but that we may gain the proper freedom towards them. Yet proper freedom—however strange this sounds—arises only where we learn to dwell on what is necessary. That comes harder to us than playing with possibilities, and so we are much less at home with praying than with wishing.

Teaching men to pray means, therefore, directing their attention to what is truly necessary. Jesus did this by means of the words of the Lord's Prayer. They are meant to give us courage to pray by directing our attention to what is truly necessary. But do they succeed with us in this? In our case do these words prove their power? Does their basic simplicity, their inescapability, their evident clarity prevail also over us? If the subject of the previous petition, our daily bread, is the epitome of all that belongs to the nurture and needs of the body, then its necessity is obvious to everyone, and can be proved if need be by the compelling force of bodily pangs. Forgiveness of debts as a necessity of existence obviously impresses itself much less forcibly on us. Here we move from the things of the body, palpable and objective, to the things of the soul, hidden and subjective. This is a realm where no general rules can be set up for everyone. Here things are not found equally convincing by everyone. One may feel one thing to be necessary for heart and conscience, another something else.

We must at all events maintain that forgiveness of debts, as distinct from what is necessary in order to live, points to that which is necessary in order to die. Certainly death has the force of that which is inevitable, of a matter of universal concern, and is irrefutably evident, at least as an unfathomable fact. But is its force so far-reaching that it fills our hearts and lays hold of our consciences not only in the immediate face of death but also daily—every single day? Does it do this in such a way that the cry, "Forgive us our debts," is one we truly utter with ultimate urgency and utter seriousness? If we are to deal with something that is always necessary, then what is necessary in order to die must prove itself to be at the same time also necessary in order to live, that is to say, the forgiveness of our debts must prove to be a necessity of existence even more urgent and more radical than the necessity of daily bread. For the latter is not needed for death, but forgiveness of debts is needed in undivided unity for both life and death —needed for life because it is needed for death, needed for death because it is needed for life.

All of us must surely admit that we are poor witnesses to the fact that the forgiveness of sins is necessary for existence. Not that we profess to be as innocent as angels! But whether, thanks to Christian training and habit, we assent as a matter of course to the necessity of forgiveness and also pray more or less regularly for it; or whether through conscientious examination of our experience, our thinking, and our conversation we have been made aware of how far we have drifted from finding overpowering reality in words like sin, guilt, and forgiveness, of how these have been devalued and become cheap currency, and of how we have to address ourselves to the seemingly endless task of discovering and regaining their true value; or whether, finally, we belong to those, or at least listen with feelings of sympathy to those, who say that all these things—God and sin, forgiveness and prayer—are dead, and who without animosity or witch-hunting, but painfully and with quiet resolution address themselves to an impoverished existence in mere this-worldliness and inexorable finitude—wherever we may belong, and were it perhaps even at the point where these different possibilities intersect, we are simply poor witnesses to the fact that the forgiveness of sins is necessary for existence. Were it not so, our talk of it must have more power, our thought about it must be closer to reality, our prayer must have more passion, our life more concentration, but also more freedom.

There is justification for warning against exalting the subject of the forgiveness of sins into a religious principle to which we dutifully struggle to aspire. And there is at least a semblance of justification for the argument that the form of innermost involvement, the way in which man is ultimately and unreservedly affected and laid hold of and is therefore also opened to the Christian proclamation, does not remain forever the same. The questions and *Anfechtung* that threatened to crush Luther as he wrestled in the monastery with the problem of standing before God were, so the argument runs, characteristic for medieval man. The Reformers' central doctrine of justification by faith alone is said to be bound up with this background and thus to be one that modern man can attain to only with difficulty. Today, it is said, man is less haunted by his sin and guilt, but is faced in a more general sense by anxiety, loneliness, and the threat of meaninglessness. A concentration on the forgiveness of sins and justification before God is held to presuppose the assurance of a law which is intelligible and unconditionally valid. But this is precisely what modern man is said to have lost. The law itself, we are told, has become questionable, and man sees himself at the mercy of a life without law, or—and this comes to the same in the end—abandoned to the tyranny of an unintelligible law.

We must not dismiss all this lightly. The objection is a warning to us against thoughtless repetition of traditional Christian phrases. Otherwise, the life-giving Gospel, which is as fresh as the morning, is turned into a musty, death-dealing law. The Christian is to speak as a witness—that is, he is to be responsible for what he says. It is only for the truth with which he is wholly one that he can allow himself, if need be, to be put to death. The prayer, "Forgive us our debts," is one we should have on our lips only when it comes from the bottom of our hearts, as a cry from the depths.

Yet I do believe it would be a fatal mistake if this petition, and with it the basic theme of the Reformers' understanding of the gospel, were taken as something of secondary importance and no longer so central for today, merely because our hearts are too sluggish to dwell attentively on it. Ultimately, after all, are we not then dwelling on what is absolutely necessary for us too? Do we not perceive what actually haunts us only when we find our way to the glowing heart of this transmitted word, thus letting it once more become a living word for us? This would take the force from the extreme objection which asks whether prayer in general, and specifically the prayer for the forgiveness of our debts, is not today an impossible thing.

One of the main facts about this petition is that here, where the right to pray at all is at stake, the impossible happens: the man who must needs fall silent before God does so by opening his mouth to God. The man who has no right to appear in God's presence comes into that presence. The man whose own verdict on himself is that he does not will what God wills and does not will that God should even exist, appeals to God to pass a verdict which contradicts and annuls this fact. Those who confess that they do not understand this petition might well be closer to it than those who take it as a matter of course.

Our understanding will be aided if we take up an apparently external peculiarity which attaches to this petition of the Our Father. Only in this petition is a concise formula expanded by the addition of a further clause: "as we also have forgiven our debtors." This, especially in its literal translation in the past tense, might appear to be a condition on which the divine forgiveness depends—or to put it in still sharper terms, an anterior achievement on man's part which obliges God to act in the same way. But that would not accord with the facts with which we are dealing here. Forgiveness is essentially pure grace, and there can be no question of its cause lying in some achievement which earns it. Even forgiveness between man and man would not be properly understood if it were placed in the category of an achievement. The man who really forgives from the heart has been evidently liberated from the vicious circle of action and reaction in which we normally find ourselves; he has made room for a totally different kind of action which he himself has experienced as a gift. Hence it is not satisfactory to put the two in the opposite order either, as if our forgiving were merely something supplementary demanded of us as a result of our receiving forgiveness. For strictly speaking it is not a second step. The man who gratefully rejoices in forgiveness received, cannot do anything other than to let others also take part in it.

The attempt to force the relationship between these two clauses into a temporal scheme fails to see that it is not a question here of isolated and accidental acts, but of a totally new situation in which everything is different from before. Since they belong so closely together it is also necessary to beware of speaking of two different dimensions which can be related to each other only by way of comparison: debts towards God and debts towards our fellow men. In any serious sense there is no such thing as a debt towards our fellow men which is not also a debt towards God. And there is no debt towards God which does not also involve our fellow men. If God is not a religious appendage to the world but rather its Creator and Lord, then the fact that we have fellow men and the fact that we have a relation to God are inseparably bound up together. Our debts towards our neighbor and our debts towards God form one single tangle of debt.

And yet, even though they belong inseparably together, we have to notice a difference. It is because of this difference that the additional clause stands here as a help towards understanding, dragging us, so to speak, headlong into the action of this petition. What the parables are in the preaching of Jesus, the clause "as we also have forgiven our debtors" is in this prayer of Jesus. It is remarkable, the way we are included here. The easiest way of giving emphasis and concrete shape to our debts towards God would surely be to remind us of our debts over against our fellow men. Who could then exclude himself as if he were not affected? From being behind in our correspondence to capital crimes there is a whole wide range of ways in which we have our fellow men on our conscience and feel their accusing eye upon us. Even though this would catch us in a grip which none of us could escape, the fact, nevertheless, is that we are in this phrase cited not as the *debtors* of our fellow men but as their *creditors*. Why? Obviously, in helping us to understand this petition this phrase cites us as witnesses—as witnesses for God and at the same time as witnesses against ourselves. That sounds mysterious and contradictory. But the fact which comes to light here is as simple as can be.

The nature of debt is surely not by any means known to us only from the perspective of the debtor, but it is usually much more exact and more poignant from the perspective of the creditor. We need have no hesitation in using a commercial illustration of this, even as Jesus also did on occasion. Suppose we have lent someone money—in good faith, as the saying goes. And now, whether from unfortunate circumstances or because the debtor is a rogue, he proves unable to pay. We have been cheated and deceived. Our legal claim and, worse still, our trust have been impaired. Where debt arises we have to think not only of penal consequences or pangs of conscience on the debtor's side, but primarily of the harm done to the creditor, the loss inflicted on him. But perhaps it would be best to drop the commercial illustration at this point. It is true that men in general are especially sensitive to financial loss. On the other hand, those who are not directly involved probably think a creditor is usually rich and there is no need to be sorry for the rich when they suffer loss. Yet the basic structure which we have noticed re-

curs in all relationships involving debt.[1] We may think—
to be content with a single example—of the deceived
husband. The loss inflicted by a debt is ultimately always
broken confidence.

And now let each of us consider how this happens to
him. Does he not then become, all against his will, a witness for God? At least in regard to what man's debts
mean for God, and thus to what is ultimately brought
about by debt? It is said that the first half of the Lord's
Prayer has to do with God, and the second half with us
men. That is only superficially true. As the first petitions,
in giving expression to the things of God, already pertain
to man, so the later petitions go on to speak of the things
of God by giving expression to the things of man. The
petition for our daily bread is concerned with God's acts
of creation and preservation. And the petition for the forgiveness of our debts? Surely with the distress of God, the
suffering of God!

But now, the testimony which we give on the basis of
our experience as deceived creditors also brings up a second point. This experience is a challenge. We cannot
then leave matters as they stand, but the attitude we adopt
when challenged by another's debt shows our capacities
as persons. One rages, another swallows it; we go to law,
or resign ourselves to the inevitable. But whether we go
to court or renounce our legal claims, our natural basic
attitude is always the same: we judge and condemn, cen-
sure and annihilate. And we even derive moral support for
ourselves from the moral defeat of our neighbor. That is

[1] [It should be noted that the German world *Schuld* means both
debt and guilt.—Translator.]

putting it briefly and crudely. But in actual life it is usually cruder still, though very often it is all extremely subtle and veiled—yet still without any fundamental change. Is it not a fact that from our painful experience of being deceived creditors we deduce the right to behave as little gods—breathing wrath and threats, as high and mighty judges?

The Bible says the root of sin is seeking to be like God. The truth of that is confirmed in the way we try to cope with things when for once we are in the right in relation to our neighbor and are aware of his debts towards us. We then become witnesses against ourselves. "Judge not, that you be not judged," says Jesus. "For with the judgment you pronounce you will be judged, and the measure you give will be the measure you get" (Matt. 7:1-2). According to Jesus' testimony, we are the image of God not in being in the right and in judging, but in suffering wrong and forgiving. That is what it means truly to be like God: not to imitate God in his majesty—the majestic God whom we do not know since as such he is hidden from us, and of whom we at best make idolatrous images—but to follow God in his humility, in his suffering, the incarnate, crucified God, to whom we can appeal when we pray, "Forgive us our debts, as we also have forgiven our debtors."

Yes, we also! This must not on any account be swallowed up in the opposite truth to which we usually testify, that we do *not* forgive our debtors. There is also this other fact, that we become free from the wrongs done to us and the rights asserted by us, free for our neighbor, our brother, in all his debts. As creditors who insist on our rights, who fail our debtor in his distress, we are, so to speak, creditors in debt—the debt (guilt) of perpetuating the other's debt, of allowing his debt to triumph over him, of not snatching him out of its hands but only driving him the more firmly into its clutches, of not making him free but casting him into jail, as debt's jailers and hangmen. How is it possible to become so free from the power of debt that—precisely when we are in the right—we are not the minions of debt but actually free the debtor from his debts? Wherever one man forgives another, and were it even noly the imperfect beginnings of forgiveness, there a miracle happens—and that of course does not mean a piece of magic, but on the contrary it means the breaking of the spell, an act of liberating power which is God's doing alone and in which we participate solely in faith, by surrendering ourselves to the miracle of forgiveness.

Is this not to dwell on what is necessary? In all our life together as men, in the private and the public sphere and all the way to the ill-starred realm of world politics, what problem could be more urgent than forgiveness, liberation from the infernal curse of debts and of the casting up of debts, of broken trust and of increasingly obdurate mistrust, of indictments and threats, censures and punishments? What does the world need more than the power that overcomes this curse of debt? And that, rightly understood, means: what does it need more than the word of God and faith? For the reality of debt and the reality of forgiveness are too vast and at the same time too mysterious to be mastered by man with his calculating mind and his achievements of power in manufacturing and technology. Here is something which, on the contrary, concerns man in the realm of his accountability and his conscience—as one who is summoned to be still and listen, and to endure the strain of his impotence under the power of the word of God. Only so does the nature of debt and the nature of forgiveness become completely clear.

Debt—that is something essentially irreversible and irreparable, in the face of which the debtor is absolutely powerless, and the reality of which he learns in the experience of being pursued by judgment—a judgment not merely on this or that, but on himself, his person. The judgment by which man stands or falls is ultimately the most real thing of all in human existence.

There is, therefore, one thing and one alone that is a match for debt: even forgiveness. Forgiveness is the verdict of acquittal; it is liberation by word. True, there also follows the duty and the power to do better or, what is more, to make good. But we can make good only a loss, not a debt. No punishment can really atone for our debts. True atonement, i.e., reconciliation, comes only through forgiveness. Hence what human existence needs most of all is the word that acquits.

The word that acquits, that confers freedom, that creates freedom, is the word that bestows faith. Debt, guilt, deals destruction to good faith. Sin is at bottom unbelief. For sin and guilt mean the destruction of fellowship. But fellowship between man and man lives from faith. Hence the relation between man and man depends ultimately on the relation between man and God. Forgiveness, not merely forgetting, not mere superficial pardon, but powerful forgiveness that annihilates the debt, is possible only to the word that opens the way to faith. For faith is a new kind of being, an existence in innocence, in innocence that is conferred by word and embraced in faith.

By all means then, let us dwell on this most necessary thing of all, with the help of the prayer which Jesus taught us: "Forgive us our debts, as we also have forgiven our debtors."

SEVEN

LEAD US NOT INTO TEMPTATION

The sixth petition of the Lord's Prayer appears to harmonize little with the spirit of the pre-Christmas season. Yet it is always the right time to pray the Our Father, and it is also always the right time to dwell on a single petition and probe its depths. We can allow it all to depend on the particular way in which this petition affects us at the present juncture and in our present mood. The particular hour that has struck and the particular way the heart beats will in any case be different for each of us. If we were now to start ringing together like bells, on different notes according to our several conditions and feelings, we would hear not merely festive chimes, but also shrill dissonances. Yet even if each of us were to sound only on his own, many of the tones would surely by themselves be false and out of tune.

We certainly do not wish to impugn the so-called Christmas spirit; we wish rather to give it full scope in as uninhibited and genuine a way as possible. Yet neither in its good sense nor in its questionable forms does the Christmas spirit supply the text to which we are bound. It is merely part of the changing situation of our lives, and this very flux makes us constantly dependent on a word that is superior to our immediate situation. It may be, paradoxically, that it is particularly difficult in the Christmas season to let the text of God's word be heard in its superiority, and to be still before it so that we can ponder it in our hearts as Mary is said to have done. That would be the only way both to pay real attention to him in whose honor the coming feast is held, and to become truly aware of the gift which God imparts to us in him. The ancient church order fosters this attentiveness and awareness by recalling for us on the Fourth Sunday in Advent the figure of John the Baptist, who seems to be so little like Christmas. Let us now stimulate our pre-Christmas attentiveness and awareness by calling to mind this petition: "Lead us not into temptation."

In *one* respect this word has an immediate appeal for us. Who is unaffected by the catchword "temptation"? There is very good reason for calling it a "catchword." It catches and stings us at our most sensitive point. That can be seen even in the weary aversion that will hear nothing of it. To desire to know nothing of temptation is obviously also a kind of temptation. To be sure, it is questionable whether this general awareness is also accompanied by a proper understanding of what temptation really is. We are compelled to reflect on this by the fact that in another respect the words, "Lead us not into temptation," are very strange. However strong their appeal to us, the real point of these words is surely that we use them to appeal to God. But what does it mean to say *to God,* "Lead us not into temptation"?

Whatever the more precise definition of "temptation" may be, it is surely something that is not good. That is why we pray against it. But the strange thing is, that by praying to God not to lead us into temptation, we indirectly give expression to the fear that he just might do it. But can it be called praying to God with trust and unshakable assurance, when at the same time a note of mistrust accompanies in the idea that perhaps we must expect the opposite from God? Indeed, is not the negative form of the petition, the only one of its kind in the Lord's Prayer, in itself already suspect? For instead of heartfelt assent to what God wills and does, we stay his arm, so to speak; we presume to know what he *might* will, and try to divert him from what he *might* do.

It is true that this petition teaches us to take refuge in God in matters of temptation. But the wording of the petition teaches us that it is also necessary at the same time to pray against God himself, and thus, as Luther was wont to say, to flee from God to God. That indeed most sharply expresses the fact that we are endangered by something for which we ourselves are not in any way a match. The temptations which come to view here are obviously not those against which it is appropriate to make a moral appeal to our strength of will; rather, the temptation which appears here is one in the face of which prayer alone is appropriate, that is, the temptation for which God alone is a match. That this involves "God alone" in the most stringent sense of the words is underlined by the fact that the endangering power of such temptation appears also to be the power of God. That is why God has to be called out against God, if there is to be any further hope here at all. But would it not then be just as correct to say that we have reached the complete end of all hope when God has to be appealed to against God, when God stands against God?

Attempts have therefore been made to resolve the contradiction and tone down the strangeness of this petition. Thus, for example, some have laid the accent on the withstanding of temptation, for which they say God is willing to give us the strength. This idea is of course in substance undeniably true. Yet it does not get to the bottom of this petition, but rather shifts its meaning. We should then really have to say: lead us out of temptation! Or even in apparent contradiction to that: lead us into temptation so that we may be tested and proved! Another way of toning the petition down is to interpret God's action here as mere permission so that it is not really in place to say to God, "Lead us not into temptation," but rather, "Suffer us not to fall into temptation." But—are we not always already in the midst of it? And above all, is what God permits also his will? If we take God seriously as God, can we here in any way evade the terrifying conclusion that God could confront us as our enemy, as the one who causes us to fall? And is it not a wonder above all wonders when, in spite of everything, what this petition hopes for actually happens—when God spares us, sets us on our feet, shields us against himself?

In face of the unfathomable depths of this petition we must now start all over again, and ask: what *is* "temptation"? This word, from its traditional use in our language, has a definite air about it and smacks, so to speak, of the moral and religious world. It is true that it sometimes also has a completely profane use, as when we say it was a sheer temptation to us to do such and such. But then there is still an implied relation of some sort to the realm of morals. Moreover, we are more or less consciously playing with the figurative application of a word borrowed from the religious sphere. We know very well that talk of temptation in the real sense has its proper home where there is a knowledge of God.

There is a negative as well as a positive side to the stamp still visibly borne by the word "temptation." If we do not trace it into the depths of the biblical witness, but stop at the platitudes of everyday use, then we succumb to a mixture of the moral and the religious in which both are out of focus. Religion becomes a special kind of morality, and morals become a preserve of religion. And together both are thus reduced to a particular way of living that cannot have any universal binding force. Religion then appears to be a private realm for those with religious inclinations, and that which is avowedly moral appears as the domain of rigorists. Under the spell of this outlook, temptation is seen as incitement to moral lapses which are usually seen only in terms of particular and specially favored aspects of the moral life. Those, however, who are not at home in an atmosphere of this kind, see "temptation" as a typical concept of a timid and petty legalism to which they consider themselves superior.

Our task here is not to choose between these two fronts. We must press beyond the usual superficial understanding of temptation to the rudiments of the matter, and advance to the point where we face the question not merely of the controversiality of a way of life, but of man himself. Man's situation is not adequately characterized by saying that as long as he lives he must be a fighter. He is at war in a

much deeper sense in that he is his own enemy. Temptation makes actual man's deliverance into his own hands,
literally in one instance (fall) after another, finally bringing about a complete fall,[1] his own undoing. Thus temptation reveals itself ultimately in the agony of being left
to oneself. To be abandoned by God and men is to be
abandoned by the protection which man needs against
himself. Thus in his agony man reveals himself as one
who relies on himself and is therefore abandoned.[2]

Viewed from the standpoint of temptation, innumerable
aspects of the contradictions of our human nature emerge.
In temptation our freedom becomes the means of our en-
slavement. It is informative to consider the contact between the word "temptation," with its peculiar moral and
religious sound, and one of the basic words of modern man,
"trial." Man has learned to make unlimited use of his
freedom in trial and experiment where he exercises the
dominion by which he makes things subject to himself,
calculable and available to his command. He puts them
to the test, cross-examines them so to speak, in such a way
that they have to divulge their secrets and show what one
can expect of them and what one can promise oneself
from them.

The first thing that strikes us here is the distinction:
man can only make something outside himself, or some
part of himself, into the object of his trial and experiment
—never, however, himself. When applied to himself, trial

[1] [There is an untranslatable wordplay here: the German word
Fall means both fall and instance.—Translator.]

[2] [Another untranslatable wordplay: in the active voice *verlassen*
can mean to rely, whereas the passive means to be abandoned.—
Translator.]

turns into a very different matter. That is shown by the very fact that we must describe this with the passive voice. We must say not that he tries (tempts)[3] himself, but that he *is* tempted, temptation befalls him, he suffers temptation. Temptation comes to him from without. Yet external things by their abundance or their shortage, by their fascinating or their repelling character, surely are involved at most only as means and occasions of temptation. Their seductive power would be nothing, if we did not give them this power by being available to temptation. And yet the "from without" does not change all over again into a "from within." However little the power of temptation ultimately lies in things, and however much it lives by our own authorization and consent, we still experience it as something that comes from without, that falls suddenly upon us—not indeed imperiously but questioningly or invitingly, not doing us violence but rather challenging us to rely precisely on our freedom.

Why is it so pertinent to notice that man is not his own tempter, but that the tempter rather approaches him from outside? Certainly not because this relieves us of our responsibility, but because it is a case of an exercise of human freedom by which man enters into slavery, selling himself to foreign masters who lord it over him.

But now, from the meaning and intent of this domination, that which is common to the way man makes things the object of his trials and experiments and to the way the tempter tries man becomes clear. Here too it is a question

---

[3] [The train of thought here is clearer in German, where the same word *versuchen* means both to try, put to the test, experiment on, and also to tempt.—Translator.]

of finding out by experiment (and that now means by temptation) what the object compelled to give information (and that is now man) shows himself to be, what he promises, what may be expected of him, whether and how far he can be relied upon. And here too the aim is to make man calculable and so to have control over him. Yet this time—because it is a case of *man* and not of some *thing* or other—the aim is totally different: not to turn him to useful purpose, but to have him ruined, to bring about his fall.

For the tempter makes it clear that we men are not to be relied upon when we rely on ourselves. What we promise is nothing other than that we shall fail. And we have no right to lay that to someone else's charge, for we are given our rights when we ourselves are the accused. It is surely the essential nature of effective temptation that in order to gain this or that we lose ourselves; by standing on our rights we forfeit our rights and so supply willy-nilly the evidence for the prosecutor in the proceedings against us. That life is a process is true in a much deeper sense than the biological one. Life is a process in the legal sense, for we have here a question of the verdict on man, who now has given his tempter the right to become his accuser, and whose efforts to defend himself break down in that they lay bare his own lack of credibility.

It is remarkable how deception and disclosure, truth and falsehood, are intermingled here. In temptation man succumbs to an illusion, and precisely thus makes the truth about himself known. And the tempter, of whom it is said that he is a liar and a murderer, does his work as accuser by telling the truth. It is no less remarkable how

116

being and not being are here intertwined. We have already said that man relies on himself and is therefore abandoned. But this abandonment does not mean simply that what has abandoned him is now not there. The afflicted man is not left alone in the sense that he is left in peace. The world is there, his fellow men are there, God is there. But in what way are they there for the afflicted man? Precisely by being there not *for* him but *against* him, not as defenders but as witnesses for the prosecution. They are there in such a way as to leave him in the lurch, present in such a way as to make him feel their absence.

For what is the real meaning of this talk about the tempter who becomes accuser? Does it mean to "paint the devil on the wall"?[4] Yes, it could well be put that way: the devil is, so to speak, the painting, in some respects the terribly true and striking painting that fills the naked wall behind which we are abandoned and left alone with ourselves, the wall of our prison, the wall through which the absence of God becomes crushingly present and our own lonely presence changes into the experience of being ourselves absent from light and warmth, fellowship and life, hope and love.

Ought we, then, to believe *in* the devil? Oh no! That would be self-contradictory. We ought in faith to trample the devil underfoot. For the devil is the offspring of unbelief. The more profoundly we grasp the truth of this, the clearer it becomes that the reality, the power, and the right behind what is experienced in all this, in temptation and affliction, is ultimately God himself—but God as he is ex-

---

[4] [German for: "Speak of the devil and he's sure to appear."— Translator.]

perienced in unbelief. Temptation, ultimately, is purely and simply a question of self-assertion in unbelief, which is the denial of God. Our unbelief is the ultimate reason for our own incredibility. And the despair in which God himself is experienced as one who is incredible and who sets the crown to our unbelief, is the uttermost depth of affliction.

"Lead us not into temptation" is thus a cry from the depths, a prayer not invented by the man in despair but taught to him and put on his lips: Confront us not, O God, so that our unbelief is punished by your becoming for us yourself the source of unbelief. Be to us the source of faith. It is true that we are in temptation and remain in temptation as long as we live. But temptation goes to work with all its deadly force, as the power of hopelessness, only when you abandon us, O God, and thereby lead us into the uttermost depth of affliction.

And now the question is put to us: are we really so serious about the Christmas message that it can become for us the source of immeasurable joy? It proclaims to us the coming of Jesus as the answer to the prayer, "Lead us not into temptation." For Jesus came for no other reason than to give us courage to believe, which means letting God be God. In Jesus God does not show us his absence in the shape of a merciless wall, but he proves his presence through his word which shatters our loneliness and which, because it transposes us into the realm where God is reliable, gives us a share in his credibility—the word to which, in the face of our accuser, we can appeal for justification.

Whether the sixth petition has helped us to an attentiveness appropriate to the pre-Christmas season will show itself in quite simple ways:

First, in whether we now really make room for joy, sheer joy which is neither obscured by the earthly joys which have attached themselves to the festival of Christmas and in which we should also rejoice, nor by the sorrow which does not disappear because of a festival and over which a festival cannot prevail.

Further, in whether we allow Christmas to be not the festival of illusion, but the festival of faith, i.e., whether we see our Savior in him who for our sakes himself suffered temptation, and who becomes the author and finisher of our faith only as we do not seek to evade our cross and affliction, but take them upon us in the certainty that God is faithful and will not let us be tempted beyond our strength, but with the temptation will also provide the way of escape in such a way that we may be able to endure it (I Cor. 10:13).

And finally, in whether we also have sympathy with the weaknesses of our fellow men, as Jesus has with our weaknesses. If anyone has even only an inkling of what it means to suffer the affliction of loneliness, to be abandoned by God and man, and if his joy in Jesus makes him no longer alone, then let him keep a look out in these days for the lonely and afflicted, taking an interest in them, speaking a kindly word, sacrificing something of time and comfort, passing on the light that has shone on us. This shows whether we are serious about the joy of Christmas.

EIGHT

DELIVER US FROM EVIL

There are some words that are like an inn.

An inn is best known by the wanderer who has no permanent abode, the homeless, the refugee. No luxury hotel awaits him. For the luxury hotel lives by being exclusive, that is, by shutting out everything that recalls the misery of the world. An inn, however, is in its purest form a shelter for the homeless, a lodging for those who must go further on their way. It is not journey's end, but is, all the same, a place to stop and draw breath. It is scantly equipped, but the barest necessities here become almost heaven on earth—bread and drink, warmth and a place to lie down. We are spoiled, so to us this sounds overdone. But millions today do not have even these bare necessities; they live in a world without inns.

The fact that there are some words which are like an inn turns our usual ideas completely upside down. On the contrary, so we think, it is man who is the inn for words. He takes them up into himself, only to let them go again —to his neighbor, or into oblivion. To be sure, he is in most cases not just a megaphone. What man hears is transformed within him and variously reshaped. We know many who are so good at this that we are reminded of a factory ceaselessly producing words, or of a warehouse with a great store of words. Yet that does not alter the basic idea that man is a sort of transit camp for words, and they are at his disposal like goods or money. The man who has an assured standing in life and is master of his situation is not at a loss for words. The man who is short of words feels himself inferior. Nevertheless, let anyone have an earth-shaking experience so that the ground rocks under his feet, then words fail him and, as we say, he becomes speechless.

In this situation we can begin to sense what the reversal of our usual ideas may mean. When a man becomes speechless from plunging into the depths, when life confronts him in such a way that he no longer knows what to say to it, when he finds everything meaningless, when God and the world become unintelligible to him and thus he necessarily also becomes unintelligible to himself, then the only thing that can still help him, if anything at all can, is a word that picks him up and takes him in, one he does not pocket like a newly found coin, but, on the contrary, a word in which he himself can find a refuge where he is safe, where he can recover his balance and find his feet. We live so much in the midst of self-evident things, that we completely fail to notice how much our lives depend *on* self-evident things. The things we superficially and falsely consider self-evident obscure the things that are impalpably, but really and truly, self-evident and by which we are upheld without knowing it. But there is provision aplenty for us to meet startling, disquieting, terrifying experiences which enable us to have at least some inkling of how a word can become an inn and resting place on our journey and can be experienced as protection, as comfort, and also as a source of new courage.

Words of prayer are intended to be understood and used as such inns, and we are expected to enter them as those who are threatened and yet secure, who are harassed and yet ever again find rest, who are weary and nevertheless refreshed. It is no doubt the summary character of this last petition of the Lord's Prayer—the fact that all that oppresses us is summed up in the one word "evil," and likewise everything we pray for in the one verb "deliver"— which precisely here enables us to see this "stopping at a wayside inn" as a basic feature of all prayer: the sense of being repeatedly and provisionally freed from evil. For although this petition, which concentrates so on "evil" in the singular, has its eye on a unique, comprehensive, and conclusive event—that is, on the end and goal, on home and not on some distant temporary stopping place—nevertheless, precisely *because* it points so decisively to that end, it is itself rightly used as a prayer only when it becomes a real inn to us here in our present existence—that is to say, only when it already begins to offer and confer the deliverance for which it has us pray and hope.

Now it must be admitted that to preach on this text is a curious thing: it is like standing at the door of this inn, to invite people in. Is that at all a sensible and hopeful thing to do? Surely the door stands open for everyone. Those who feel the need will come soon enough. But those who are not yet ready to come in should surely be allowed to go their way. If it is necessary to propagandize and push this petition, then the only thing capable of doing it, so it seems, would be the very evil which plagues and batters men until they are ready to take refuge in this petition, "Deliver us from evil." Ought we to wish for that and long for it? In order to gain recognition for this petition among men, ought we secretly to interpose another petition, "Plague them with evil," and as propaganda agents for the gospel use that as a sort of trap or ambush?

It is the homeless wanderer's situation itself which teaches him to make use of the inn. Surely the only thing that can teach us rightly to pray this petition is the situation it presupposes. The man who is drowning will shout for help soon enough. One ought not to shout when there is no danger. No one should require either himself or anyone else to pray, "Deliver us from evil," unless the prayer comes from the heart like a cry from the depths. Or ought it to be our job to make the contented discontented, to convince those who are happily going their way that they are really in bad shape, that their home is not a home at all, their happiness no real happiness, and their life even at its best a vale of tears?

It may be that there is no need to be so concerned about the joy of the glad and the happiness of the happy. If it is genuine, then it will not allow itself to be troubled or destroyed. Yet where do we ever meet pure joy and unclouded happiness? Should we not rather be concerned that there is so much misuse of this petition which appeals without any qualification or closer definition to men's ideas about, and desires for, liberation from evil? Should we not be concerned that, in terms of our picture, the inn is filled with all kinds of people who are not at all in danger and merely want to get by cheaply? Ought the preacher not rather to stand before the inn like a Cerberus and bar entrance? Mere toothache, he might say for example, does not confer on anyone the right to make use of this petition. Neither does lovesickness, or the evil consequences of our own folly. Only those who are exercised by the tribulations of the end and who long for the joys of heaven, who have no more interest in the world and are filled only with spiritual hunger for eternity—only they have a right to this prayer.

We are not exactly living in an age when prayer is used to excess. The question is rather, who still prays at all? Yet it is of no matter whether the great mass of people prays or, comparatively speaking, only a rapidly decreasing minority. Each of us is in any event still compelled to ask himself whether this is really the proper place for him: whether in all his particular burdens, worries, and anxieties, in everything that sticks in his throat and that rouses in him only the single desire to get away from it all—whether in face of all that, and under the burden of all that, he should resort to this particular resting place, to this word, "Deliver us from evil."

One might think our picture was badly chosen. Such a word as this prayer is surely more like a stately church than a profane inn, and therefore suited for people in their Sunday best and with their Sunday sentiments, rather than for those who bear the stains and cares of everyday. Or it is for those who rise to the vast and lofty thoughts of the Bible concerning time and eternity, heaven and earth, God and the world; and not for those who are tied up in the realm of their own little, narrow, private life and experience. And yet the simple fact is that the things which directly concern and exercise us, harass and plague us, hurt us and make us cry out—the things that make us long to escape the present and be free for a better future are the ordinary, crude things of everyday. Do they give us a right to pray?

They do indeed: the door is open to all without distinction, and this inn has room for everyone. To expound the petition, "Deliver us from evil," is not to narrow it down but to broaden it out until everyone has access to it, whatever the distress that plagues him, whatever the longings that move him. To everyone who is engaged in this attempt to escape forward into the future—and who is not! —this word offers a ready reception for his longings, his sighs, his tears, his sense of being at his wits' end. Magnitude is of no consequence. We ought not artificially to manufacture distresses for ourselves, but ought honestly to face up to those we really have, even when to the eye of the general public they are merely private bagatelles. The fundamental condition of prayer is the will to be honest. Therefore we should come as we are. The question then becomes whether we shall go away again as we were.

Whatever it may be that makes us say, "Deliver us from evil," in order to find shelter from all the things which haunt us, we must not in any event enter into these words halfheartedly without taking account of where we find ourselves. The first thing to be said then would be: we do not find ourselves alone. This is to begin with no comforting discovery. It is like our disappointment at finding a large dormitory waiting for us instead of a private room. The man who seeks refuge in the prayer, "Deliver us from evil," must not expect any preferential treatment and must not forbid admission to anyone else; he must in-

deed reconcile himself to the discovery that here he meets
even those who do not explicitly pray this prayer on their
own, but who are living commentaries on it, whose distress and oppression cries to heaven, "Deliver us from
evil."

Whoever concerns himself with this prayer must concern himself first of all with the word "us." That is the
first change that comes over us in this inn. It is true that
we remain as we are, with all our, perhaps very paltry,
troubles. And yet we do *not* remain as we are, insofar as
we now find ourselves in a different environment. My situation is not the only situation covered by this prayer. I
suddenly find myself confronted by an infinite society of
sufferers in which I am but a drop in the ocean. I simply
cannot help observing all that is there before my eyes and
ears—men in concentration camps, lovers cruelly separated by a wall, children who are starving. There is no
knowing where to start and where to stop when it comes
to counting up those who are embraced by this petition,
all who find a lodging in this inn!

If our hearts and minds are awake as we cast ourselves
and our fate upon this word, "Deliver us from evil," then
we become contemporaries of all who suffer and cry out
for deliverance. Then we cannot say, "What are the starving masses in India to me?" Then we become contemporary even with things that seem to belong to the past,
such as the gas chambers of Auschwitz—but how could
such a thing ever become a thing of the past? A sea of
torment wells up around us. We are encompassed by
waves of unbearable horror. Our ears must ring with the
screams of the desperate, and our breath must stick in our

throats before the silence of those now dumb forever. As contemporaries of the suffering, we are also their fellows in suffering. When we say, "Deliver us from evil," then we simply cannot exclude anyone, and we beseech deliverance not merely for each from his own distress, but for each from the distress of all. For in this inn we are all one. How could the prayer be heard for me and not for the others? The suffering of my neighbor is also mine. And when I say, "Deliver us from evil," then I am speaking in the name of all, in the name of the world.

Does that mean that what should have been our inn now becomes a hell? How can we bear what the realization of this "us" imposes on us? And who can comprehend this anyway? The more massive the number of sufferers, the more abstract becomes our fellowship in suffering. We are told that every second two or three people in the world die of hunger. We are appalled, and yet pass on to everyday things. It would be a different matter if we were condemned to witness one man starve to death and not be able to help. We certainly ought not to flee from this prayer's urge towards universality, and therewith also from its boundless reach, but we do need to avoid wandering off into abstractions, statistics, inurement. When the suffering of the whole world surges around us, we must not allow it to make us forget the concrete ways in which we ourselves experience that suffering. Then do toothache, lovesickness, and the evil consequences of our own folly have a place in this prayer after all? They certainly do! But here too it is essential to expose ourselves to the transformation which takes place. For now the concept of evil begins to disclose its abysmal depths.

A remark on the wording of the petition may be made here. When I came as a first-year student to Marburg and learned that in one church the service was Lutheran and in another Reformed and when I asked my landlady about the difference, she explained that in the one they say, "Deliver us from ill" (*Übel*), and in the other, "Deliver us from evil" (*Bösen*). That, to be sure, was undeniable. But as a lesson on the confessions it was merely a confirmation of the way Christians are mostly divided—by questions of custom and not by the question of truth. For while we can see that the (Reformed) translation, "from evil," is preferable because it includes not merely all kinds of ills of body and soul but also moral evil, and even makes possible a personal interpretation of the devil himself, it must also be observed that Luther prudently and considerately left the wording in the form people had been accustomed to since the Middle Ages, while in his exposition giving full and vigorous emphasis to the relation of evil to the archenemy of God.

So this need not detain us. Wherever we start, we are taken the whole way. If we begin with a single bodily ill from which we are suffering, and consider why we want to be rid of it, why it makes us impatient, perhaps even nasty, or how it will be when we are freed from it and what is to be expected from the sort of deliverance we long for, then we soon find ourselves in the midst of a whirlpool in which we recognize two things: first, that we ourselves give evil its power by the way we deal with it, the way we try to compensate for it and cure it, the way we fear it and flee from it, all because we are enslaved to our fears, or, more pointedly, we are enslaved to our own self-seeking. And secondly, that we are in league with *the* power which, apart from any guilt that can be charged to individuals, has the world in its clutches and is described in the New Testament as the god of this age, the god of this world. Not merely all sufferers on earth belong together in this petition; all the forms in which evil manifests itself also belong here. In this inn we are transformed into the midst of the whole, turned to face the end, set in a context that concerns not merely our little life and experience but the whole world's history, even though we do not know its direction. But this we do know: we cannot pray, "Deliver us from evil," without the end of all evil coming into view.

But it is just here not only that so many of our contemporaries bristle, but also that something in all of us also bristles against entering completely into this petition. For what gives us the assurance to pray like this? What makes this petition not only the place where we find all the unbearable things of the world marshalled in an unbearable mass before our eyes, but also and above all the place where the incomprehensible goodness and mercy of God triumphs in incomprehensible ways? What after all does it mean to "deliver"? Is *that* liberation when I am freed from one burden in order to have another put in its place? Is *that* deliverance when we have survived one deadly peril but others are still ahead? Is *that* redemption when ultimately death awaits us? Is *that* gospel, glad tidings of the Redeemer, when he is one who hangs on a cross?

We shall learn to pray this prayer in truth only when we allow our ideas and claims about redemption to undergo a transformation, only when we do not secretly interpret the resurrection of the dead as a triumph of our earthly life, as the fulfillment of our longing for self-preservation. The gospel of Jesus Christ does not promise us freedom from death. It promises us only—but what do we mean by "only" here?—that because of Jesus death is no longer death, that even death cannot separate us from the love of God.

This means today that since God is for us, we are free from all evil, so far as we believe the call of Jesus—free in that we now do battle with an enemy who still assails us and seeks to separate us from the love of God, free in prayer and hope, free in the refuge provided even now in the midst of this world by the petition, "Deliver us from evil," an inn that gives us assurance of our future home.

And what will it mean then? That we do not know, because it is not a matter of knowledge; it can only be a matter of faith. For the fact that God is for us when everything is against us—and that certainly also means that in death there will be true life and God's sovereignty will be manifest—that is something we *believe*. But to dream of it in detail is forbidden us by the terseness of the petition, "Deliver us from evil." For only when the consummation comes, and even then, shall we be like them that dream (Ps. 126:1).

NINE

FOR THINE IS THE KINGDOM, AND THE POWER, AND THE GLORY, FOR EVER. AMEN.

This clause, so familiar to us as the close of the Lord's Prayer, is a later addition. It is omitted by the authoritative witnesses to the New Testament text. The new Zurich Bible therefore drops it to a footnote—and rightly so, from the historical point of view. Nevertheless, these words are so very right in content, that we have no reason for failing to include them when we pray the Our Father. On the contrary, we have every reason to dwell thoughtfully upon them.

For to a certain extent the whole matter is decided at the end—as happens for example also in a letter, and likewise with our lives. And yet, is that really true? These very examples would seem to prove the contrary.

What importance really attaches to the end of a letter? Mostly it is a formality. We use one of the usual patterns: "With all good wishes, Yours sincerely, John," or "Assuring you of our best attention at all times, Yours faithfully, So-and-so." In exceptional cases we may perhaps succeed for once in giving a letter a decisive turn by the concluding phrase. But how good that we do not have to try that every time! How embarrassing it is when someone strains to be original! How helpful, and to a certain extent protecting, forms and conventions can be in correspondence, as well as in our dealings with each other in general! We should not despise them, but rather take care of them. And part of that is recognizing the need they fill.

Why, after all, must a letter have a formal ending instead of simply stopping? We take the closing so much for granted that we only notice it when it is omitted—as when someone has forgotten to sign his name under a letter, or when a coward sends an anonymous letter, or when, in the case of an intentional insult, a mere signature is appended without any form of greeting. The closing is by no means the place to impart new information; it is there merely to make explicit once again who answers for the contents, who it is who really imparts himself in and behind all the information imparted in the letter, what is the nature of his relationship to the addressee, the degree of respect or affection in which the letter professes to be written, the sort of reception with which it hopes to meet. What stands at the end is thus what was already the tacit ground of the whole letter, but now it is once more explicitly stated and confirmed. It brings out what is of decisive importance in the letter as an event between man and man.

It is much the same with this final clause of the Lord's Prayer. It does not add still another petition to those that have gone before. It expresses nothing other than what was already definite in every preceding word. It brings the prayer to a close by voicing the courage, confidence, and assurance in which it has been prayed and, as it were, by setting the seal and signature under it. In one respect, however, this happens in a wholly different way than in a letter. Praying is a thing we cannot do in our own name. It is the exact opposite of the case in which a man himself answers for his own words. To be sure, it is supremely true that prayer is a responsible act. Yet it is a kind of responsibility in which the man who prays surrenders himself. Certainly he is asked what really gives him the right, the boldness, the confidence, to speak and call into the empty, impenetrable darkness like this. But to that he can ultimately answer only by doing it.

Those who call upon God can appeal to nothing other than God himself in vindication of their action. In his name alone is the ground of prayer and the source of its validity. And it is only in this movement of joining in the praise of God's name that the one who prays finally comes into view himself; and this happens in such a fashion that there is nothing more whatever to be said of the one who prays, but only of God, and in this very way the speaker is taken up into the word addressed to God. That is why it is profoundly significant that the concluding formula of the Lord's Prayer has the character of a later addition. It explicitly describes once more the movement of joining in the prayer which Jesus taught. It stands, as it were, at the point where everyone who adopts this prayer as his own has to do so by putting his own signature to it, thus explicitly taking responsibility for it; yet this act of appropriation becomes an act of pure response: "For thine is the kingdom, and the power, and the glory, for ever. Amen." Thus once more at the end sounds the fundamental note of the whole.

We have said that to a certain extent the decision concerning the whole thing comes at the end, and we first illustrated that by comparison with a letter. The second illustration which we set beside that one seems a great deal more to the point, namely, that it is much the same with our life itself. That the decision concerning the whole of life comes at the end sounds like pious talk. Yet what is it really supposed to mean? That death is the decisive word about life? That is admittedly and obviously the case. All things are ultimately subject to its decree. Death allows no gainsaying and no exception. But what does death really say? In what does its decision consist? What is death's word? Is not its voice silence, its decision a silence that reduces us to silence? But surely a decision about life cannot be given by what reduces life to silence, but only by that which makes it speak and brings out its truth—by that which makes life not absolutely uncertain but absolutely certain.

Death, to be sure, looks as though it were the most certain thing in life. When we want to lay strong emphasis on the certainty of anything, we say it is "as sure as death." But still, the death that is described as certain and inescapable is always the death which I observe at a distance in others, the death that is still external to myself, that has not yet closed in on me, that is not yet acute, not yet real, not yet actually experienced. Death is a thing no one can speak of from experience. When we speak of death we are speaking of something of which strictly we cannot speak—not, at all events, when we regard it as really determinative for the whole of life, and yet still go on living. For life in actual fact involves a word that in some way

136

or other supplies encouragement, gives hope, bestows certainty. Death, to be sure, awaits us, yet not as a certainty that makes us certain, but rather as a source of uncertainty. And it is only in temporary denial of death and temporary protest against death—only in clinging to the things which for a time supply some sort of courage in the face of death, confer a ray of hope, grant a glimmer of assurance—that life can exist at all. Where death prevails there is *ipso facto* no life. Life, on the other hand, is contradiction and defiance of death, perhaps flight from death, but at all events decision against death.

Now I suppose that in contrast to this sort of determined but possibly very shortsighted and short-lived will to live which defies death and seeks to flee from it, it will be considered Christian nevertheless to hold to the opinion that the decision about all of life is made at the end of life—in the sense that things primarily depend on the hour of death and how we behave then. And in view of the way death has today been banished from the public eye into the seclusion of our hospitals, and in view of the way dying has been reduced to a soulless technicality, one might certainly feel that it is high time to return again to the medieval example of practicing the *ars moriendi,* the art of dying, and so learn to master life on the basis of the proper inward mastery of death. Yet however impressive that may be, it is not at all in accord with the truth of the gospel to say that our superiority to death—and such a thing does in fact exist, as is proved by many examples, above all that of Socrates—provides the decision concerning the whole of life.

That the decision about all of life comes at the end of

life can only mean—but must quite definitely mean—that the one thing which is ultimately and certainly decisive for life is that which I do not have to revoke in the face of death, because it is a word which gives assurance and as such is a match for, and indeed superior to, the silence of death. It is a word, however, by no means decisive only at the last moment, but in every moment of life—certainly with very different degrees of urgency and audibility. We should not, and incidentally cannot, seek to live in a sort of existential tenseness as though every hour were our last hour. But because we have to go on living, we must be clear that at all times we are faced with the question of what life really is; by living we constantly give some sort of answer to the question about what it is that gives us the assurance to live. What the end of life really expresses is nothing other than what was always at stake in the midst of life, but now it is at stake in the form of a specially urgent question, one that silences every word which is not a match for the silence of death.

What was meant to be merely an illustrative comparison, namely, the relation of the end of life to life as a whole, has seemingly taken us a long way from what it was meant to illustrate, namely, the relation of the end of the prayer to the prayer as a whole. In actual fact, however, the two belong so closely together that it is not a case of a comparison at all, but of one and the same thing. Life and prayer, it is true, seem to be poles apart. Everyone has experienced—possibly only negatively— how difficult it is to bring these two together and make them a single unity. The question of time is symptomatic of the difficulty. Life, so it seems, leaves us no time for praying.

If anything, we hardly allow ourselves as much time for it as for cleaning our teeth. And the difficulty becomes even more striking with the question of the language of prayer. How we stutter and stumble when it comes to bringing prayer into intelligible contact with life, taking life up into prayer! But the difficulty is most plain—and this is surely the ground of all the rest—in the fact that life irresistably claims us through the compelling force of what is necessary and obvious: hunger and desire, tasks and disappointments, love and fear. Prayer, on the other hand, appears to be something supplementary, something we may or may not feel obliged to do.

But although in practice things seem to our eyes to be like this, in actual fact the truth about life and prayer is completely different. Rightly understood, prayer is in a certain sense life in its most concentrated form: stopping and facing up to the summons which calls us not merely to this or that, that is, to things we have to do or to achieve, but to what we *are,* in order that we should be it in very truth, and that means, before God. Because we are always already called and claimed, and in a far more radical way than, as we say, life claims us; because we are already called and claimed by the basic question that precedes and underlines all individual claims, "Adam, where are you?" . . . "Man, where are you?"—that is to say, by the question which challenges us in person, summons us to life, and at the same time summons us to ultimate responsibility—because of that, praying, as an act of standing up and answering this summons, is in actual fact the giving of our most concentrated attention to the real business of living.

The fact that praying comes so hard to us is simply due to the fact that it is so hard for us to attend with utter concentration to the summons to live. For that reason, however, the opposite is also true: life, rightly understood, is constant prayer. If prayer is responding to the call that summons us to life, then life itself, when we see it for what it truly is, is a constant act of response. We men in being summoned to life are summoned to an existence which is one of response. And so in fact existing is always responding, even when we do not know and consider either what summons we are responding to or what our response really is.

Are these merely assertions which are as far removed from living experience as prayer usually seems to us to be from real life? When we ask what a man is, we can also put the question like this: what has he to say? Is he a man who has no say? Or is he one who has something to say? That strikes at the deepest roots of human existence. But everything now depends on the standard for the authentification of what man has to say.

What it means to speak of God—and there can be speaking *of God* only when it is speaking *before* God—is identical with the meaning of prayer: man is asked what he has to say before God. He *is* and is *worth* what he has to say before God. This stands in sharpest contrast to the way we usually judge. Whether a man has any say is measured in men's eyes by the orders he can give, the extent of his sovereignty and power, the nature of the honor that accrues to him. Before God, however, the only man who has anything to say is the one who finds nothing to say about his own power and honor, his own capacities, his achievements, his glory; he is the one who has only one thing to say: "Thine is the kingdom, and the power, and the glory, for ever."

And now do not object that this just shows again how far prayer is removed from life. In life it is a very different matter: there the only thing that counts is one's own power and achievements, there what a man has to say is measured by what he can do. Indeed, I must reply, this is so as long as life is chopped up into different departments and considered in various respects. Then one man has authority and power in one respect, another in another, one has much, another little, one stands in the limelight, another in the shadows. But the right to make such distinctions is called into fundamental question when one confronts the powers which call into question both every man and mankind as a whole. What after all has any of the high and mighty among men to say to these? What can he do against such powers of destruction and darkness? What is he worth when this question is asked in strict regard to his ultimate value? Then all the self-assurance of the mighty fades away. But a man who before the world has virtually nothing to say, but is rejected and despised, trampled and martyred, can then be one who is worth something before God. And his assurance of this can make him, in spite of all his impotence before the world, the witness to a unique and strange, yet real and true, power, the witness to the fact that the kingdom, and the power, and the glory are God's.

Thus the things which appear to us to be separated here link up together. Life and prayer meet at least in this one point: in both it is a question of certainty. Life that is

utterly void of certainty is no life. Prayer without certainty
is no prayer. This makes plain that the two do not simply
stand independently side by side, but are really one. If
prayer is not to be altogether an illusion and a waste of
time, then it must be subjected to the most stringent criterion, namely, the manifold experience of uncertainty
in the real life of everyday; here must be the proving
ground for its affirmation of a certainty that makes us
certain. And it is equally true that if life is not to be an
illusion and a waste of time, then it must be subjected to
the most stringent criticism, namely, to the question of the
certainty that is superior to all uncertainty and pseudo
certainty.

Do not let us now be confused by the multitude of
questions that would here still have to be raised and considered, but let us hold to the simple, yet for that very reason inexhaustible, truth that our wretchedness—our cul-
pable wretchedness—consists in our being the prey of uncertainty. Is it not a fact that everything would be in order and all would be well, if in all that we do and are we
were only sure? Sure of whom? Why, certainly not of
ourselves, but of God—and therefore not in order to justify and glorify ourselves, but rather to glorify and praise
God as just, as true, as dependable, as faithful, as merciful.
Why and in what sense? Not in projecting to infinity
what we ourselves would like to be, but in accepting what
Jesus has taught us—taught us in the Our Father and, as
a supreme commentary on that, in his life of suffering and
death.

If we thus join in the word which is Jesus himself, then
we can no longer allow ourselves to be carried away by

foolish fantasies about all the things God really ought to do. But then we hold to what he *has done*—to the kingdom, the power, and the glory as they have been revealed in Jesus, to the yea and amen which he is to all promises, to him as the fulfillment which is already given to all our prayers and which surpasses all we ask or think.

It is actually in itself a strange thing, not so much that we pray, but rather that we can confidently stop praying. In one sense, it is true, we on earth never cease to pray. For our praying lasts as long as our life lasts. In another sense, however, we can in actual fact stop praying any time, because we have completed our prayer when we do not merely *say* "Amen," but when we *believe* it, that is, when we let God be God. Then we are also ready at any time for this life to end, so as even in death to let God be God, in the certainty that "thine is the kingdom, and the power, and the glory, for ever. Amen."

THE PREACHER'S PAPERBACK LIBRARY

Volumes already published:

1. *The Servant of the Word* by H. H. Farmer. 1964.

2. *The Care of the Earth and Other University Sermons* by Joseph Sittler. 1964.

3. *The Preaching of F. W. Robertson* edited by Gilbert E. Doan, Jr. 1964.

4. *A Brief History of Preaching* by Yngve Brilioth. 1965.

5. *The Living Word* by Gustaf Wingren. 1965.

6. *On Prayer* by Gerhard Ebeling. 1966.

Further volumes are in preparation.

Type: 11 on 13 Garamond
Display: Garamond Italics
Paper: White Standard R Antique